ENVIRONMENTAL SANITATION HEALTH AND PANCHAYATI RAJ

About the Authors

Prof. Bakshi D. Sinha, Adviser, Institute of Social Sciences, has worked for over four-and-a-half decades as Economist and Research Scholar in different universities in India and abroad as well as national and international organisations. He was educated in Bihar and Hollland. Prof. Bakshi D. Sinha has done considerable research work on urban and rural problems, macro and micro planning, development and evaluation studies. He has several publications to his credit.

Dr. P.S.K. Menon, Economist and former consultant, Planning Commission, Government of India, has over three decades of varied experiences in research and administration. Dr. Menon has served in various capacities in the Departments of Government of Madhya Pradesh and ministries of Home and Welfare, Government of India. He has published several research papers in reputed journals. His contribution to the literature on Welfare and Development of Schedules Castes and Scheduled Tribes is noteworthy.

Environmental Sanitation Health and Panchayati Raj

(Revised and Enlarged Edition)

Bakshi D. Sinha
P.S.K. Menon

Published for

INSTITUTE OF SOCIAL SCIENCES

by

CONCEPT PUBLISHING COMPANY PVT. LTD.
NEW DELHI-110059

ISBN: 978-81-7022-775-5

First Published 1996
Revsied and Enlarged Edition 2000

Published and Printed by

Concept
Since 1974

Concept Publishing Company Pvt. Ltd.
A/15-16, Commercial Block, Mohan Garden,
New Delhi-110059 (India)
T: 91-11-41101460
E: publishing@conceptpub.com, *W*: www.conceptpub.com

CONTENTS

A Message from Mulk Raj Anand

THE study of various facets of Environmental Sanitation, Health and Panchayati Raj, conducted by Prof. Bakshi D. Sinha and Dr. P.S.K. Menon for the Institute of Social Sciences, has its sources in the mature wisdom of Mahatma Gandhi, who thought out plans to uplift of our country, through development from village upwards.

Gandhiji was aware that, inspite of disruptions, wars of conquest and deprivation, in every century, the village republics had lasted out. Because, from ancient times downwards, in our tradition, the land was not owned by the raja or the ryot, but everyone had rights in land and did not own any portion of it.

Thus, when Ashoka declared *Dhama*, or social welfare, as the policy of the State, he had in mind the provisions to every village through panchayats. The renovation of Panchayati Raj involves functioning participation of people from village upwards.

The Mahatma envisaged the Ashokan *Dhama* as model for administration and reconstruction in village life by training people in Sarvodaya constructive work.

In his campaign against untouchability and sanctification of the work of cleaning dirt, the Mahatma himself got model latrines built in Sabarmati village, and, by involving his followers in cleaning latrines, Gandhiji sanctified scavenging.

If Panchayati Raj, envisaged through recent legislation, is to be realised genuinely, then the creation, in every house, of Sulabh Shauchalayas (latrines) invention for evacuation and disposal of refuse, becomes an important aspect of reform for the expanding population. Perhaps one could call it a revolution in so far as it liberates all outcastes from the rigours of the caste system.

Such development would be the basis of creating congenial environment from village upwards and inevitably make the atmosphere refreshing for young and old. Certainly, it would end the humiliation of women having to expose themselves in open fields at dawn or alternatively carry the burden of the night-soil till sunset.

I hope the book comes to the notice of governmental agencies, international organisations and local NGOs as it gives guidelines to achieve appointed goals.

If the reverse traffic of migration from urban to rural is to set in, and India wishes to have a healthy nation, such research studies will show the way to pioneer revolutionary development.

The approach of Dr. George Mathew, Director, Institute of Social Sciences, pioneers constructive thinking for practical realisation of visionary ideas.

Foreword

(First Edition)

ONE of the major areas of current concern that the Institute of Social Sciences has been investigating and deliberating on has been the role of panchayats in the field of decentralised local self-government institutions. The historic Seventy-third Amendment to the Constitution is epoch-making in its implications for the well-being of our rural population. It has been continuously orchestrated by every person of reckoning in almost all walks of life. Well, the basic structural changes needed to realise such a desirable goal, has, no doubt, been firmly established. The eagerness with which we now look forward, is the result of the Parliament's wisdom in incorporating provisions in the Constitution, making it possible for the States and other agencies in the democratic set-up, to strengthen the grassroot level institutions of working democracy to improve the quality of life of the rural people.

The twenty-nine items in the Eleventh Schedule of the Constitution and the all-pervasive Finance Commission envisaged under the Seventy-third Amendment are full of potential to usher in a sea-change in the rural scene to upgrade all essential areas of concern for improving the living standards of our rural population. Drinking water, housing, poverty alleviation programmes, health and sanitation, maintenance of community assets etc. are but a few areas where the Panchayati Raj set-up could mobilise efforts to vastly improve the status of environmental sanitation and health standards in large parts of our country, that is, rural areas.

When the Akhil Bharatiya Paryavaran Evam Gramin Vikas Sansthan (ABPEGVS), a voluntary organisation, mooted the proposal to sponsor a study on Environmental Sanitation, Health and Panchayati Raj, so dear to the Institute of Social Sciences, we readily agreed. Now the results of the study are before you. The Institute places on record its deep gratitude to ABPEGVS for sponsoring this important study.

The All-India study covering ten States and fifteen specific projects, is indeed a good effort. In this task we have had the unstinted cooperation of all concerned agencies. The search for a viable model or models to ensure environmental sanitation, health and Panchayati Raj has not yet ended.

The study team headed by Prof. Bakshi D. Sinha, ably assisted by Dr. P. S. K. Menon, worked with dedication and a sense of purpose to focus on the essential areas requiring attention. We intend to pursue vigorously some of the crucial issues emerging from the study to translate into action, the oft-repeated dictum,"from lab to field".

April 8, 1996

GEORGE MATHEW
Director

Foreword

(Revised and Enlarged Edition)

THE first edition of our book "Environmental Sanitation, Health and Panchayati Raj" was well received and the response was overwhelming as revealed from the very many reviews.

While giving a critical review of the book in *The Tribune*, September 1996, Dr. Mulk Raj Anand wrote: "this study of various facets of Environmental Sanitation, Health and Panchayati Raj has its sources in the mature wisdom of Mahatma Gandhi, who thought our plans to uplift our country to developments in villages". He stated that "at the end of 19th century... social life in cities was regulated with adequate attention, to water, light and sanitation, at least for the upper orders... which compelled Mahatma Gandhi to initiate campaign for Panchayati Raj... on the basis of Ashoka's Dhama Model for administration and prompted construction of villages by the folk themselves through Sarvodaya Movement." Dr. Anand, in the review in *Deccan Chronicles* (October 1996) wrote "villages which are Islands of Neglect will depend on the activisation of Panchayati Raj from legislation to movement, as has been achieved in model villages of South Maharashtra under the dynamic leadership of Anna Hazare." Mala Bhandari, while reviewing the book in the Journal of the Indian Sociological Society in September 1997 writes: "an interface that emerges strongly from this study is that no development programme can improve the lives of the people unless it becomes a grassroot level movement involving the local people and local resources at every stage of the programme". The Journal of the Indian Institute of Economics, *the Asian Economic Review*, noted that "the authors are optimistic in their conclusion that the Seventy-third Amendment has tremendous potential in transforming the rural scene to meet people's aspirations and needs adequately."

What the reviewers have emphasised has been amply elaborated in this book and also in *Panchayati Raj in India: From Legislation to Movement* (Concept:1995). The story of Panchayati Raj in India was well brought out by Asoka Mehta Committee (1978). In fact, the decline after 1977 in Panchayati Raj institutions was more rapid. The hopes were kindled and aspirations high with the enactment of the Constitution (Seventy-third Amendment) Act, 1992 incorporating part IX in the Constitution with regard to the panchayats and Eleventh Schedule which included 29 functions to be directly under the jurisdiction and control of the panchayats at all three levels.

The Movement, however, has not trickled down from the pious legislations so far, because of various hindrances in practically all the States. The draft Ninth Five Year Plan, document, while assessing the performance of the Eighth Five Year Plan states that "safe drinking water supply and sanitary disposal of solid and liquid wastes contributed to the continued high morbidity from water-borne and vector-borne diseases" in rural areas particularly. The document further emphasises that the universal coverage of safe-drinking water supply in each village/habitation along with environmental sanitation programmes in rural areas" should be the main thrust of the gram panchayats and its institutions. For this institutional mechanism has to be developed where villagers/communities have to be motivated not only for implementation of all programmes but also to accept responsibility of day-to-day affairs of all basic and general needs of the village communities without any external interference either of politicians, governments or bureaucrats etc. The Village Models as envisaged and implemented by Ram Krishna Mission in Midnapore District in West Bengal, Sri Satya Sai Trust of Nilayam (Puttaparty) in Andhra Pradesh and South Maharashtra by Anna Hazare should be replicated in other parts of the country for sustainable development. It must be done after studying the local conditions, and then to adopt the successful Models with desired modifications.

I would like to place on record our deep appreciation to Prof. Bakshi D. Sinha, team leader of the project who worked tirelessly to bring out the Revised and Enlarged Edition. My gratitude to Dr. P.S.K. Menon who lent his support to this project. Both Prof. Sinha and Dr. Menon command recognition for the complicated and complex task done so meticulously with constructive thinking and vision.

February 10, 1999

GEORGE MATHEW
Director

Preface

(First Edition)

THE realisation that a mere 5.58 per cent out of 623 million rural population (74 per cent of the country's total population of 839 million, as per 1991 Census) has been covered by both safe drinking water and toilet facilities – notwithstanding the fact that we have had four and a half decades of developmental planning and rural development programmes – is certainly a matter of grave concern to planners and policy-makers. To tackle these minimum needs and for raising the level of environmental sanitation and health status affecting 112 million rural households (1991 Census) a more purposeful campaign will need to be conducted. This massive task indeed calls for a re-thinking and a radical change in the concept and methodology of rural development planning in general and upgradation of environmental sanitation and health programmes in particular.

Broadly speaking, the main issue for upgradation of environmental sanitation and health status of rural people should be viewed in the context of two aspects. First, the average growth rate of the rural population (2.41 per cent per annum) as also the increase in the number of households to be provided with toilets or basic sanitation facilities along with safe drinking water supply free from biological contaminations (e.g. guineaworm, cholera, typhoid etc.) and chemical contaminations (e.g. excess fluoride, iron, arsenic, nitrate, brackishness etc.). Secondly, the legislative measures formulated in pursuance of the Constitution (Seventy-third) Amendment Act, 1992 and especially with regard to the Eleventh Schedule thereof (Article 243G). Empowerment of panchayats for governance at the grassroots with people's participation for overall rural development as also for sanitation and health services in each household and village community as a whole is a *sine qua non* for improving the environmental and health status to enhance the quality of life of rural people. It is provided under Article 243-I that a State Finance Commission be set up to review the financial position of panchayats and recommend to the appropriate authority for provision of required finances for development needs of the panchayats. It is also provided that panchayats and the village community has the right to take decisions and the freedom to levy or increase and appropriate taxes, duties, tolls and fees in accordance with the development needs and priorities of the village community and panchayats. Constitutional mandates should enable the panchayats to be lively organisations to tackle the local problems in an effective manner.

Against this background, the present study of "Environmental Sanitation, Health and Panchayati Raj" was undertaken by the Institute of Social Sciences, New Delhi. The main objectives of the study were:

(i) to assess the methods of implementation and monitoring of some experimental sanitation and health programmes in different areas of the country. These included programmes of Central and State governments as well as International Organisations (such as UNICEF, World Bank and WHO) and some Non-Governmental Organisations (NGOs) like Sulabh International Social Service Organisation (SISSO), Environmental Sanitation Institute (ESI) and the Bio-Village Model of M.S. Swaminathan Research Foundation, and

(ii) to evolve an appropriate Environmental Sanitation and Health Model synthesising the salient aspects of the existing experimental programmes suitable for adoption in the decentralised 'People's Sector' in the Panchayati Raj structure.

The methodology adopted for the study was to obtain secondary information through: (i) meetings and interviews with concerned Central and State government officials, block and panchayat functionaries, NGOs and international organisations at various levels; (ii) conducting group interviews of some beneficiaries; and (iii) field observations.

While conducting the study, I have had discussions with policy-makers, planners and officials in the concerned ministries of the Government of India, Departments of the State governments of Bihar, Goa, Gujarat, Haryana, Orissa, Rajasthan, Tamil Nadu, Uttar Pradesh, West Bengal and the Union Territory of Pondicherry as well as concerned NGOs/implementing agencies. I thank them sincerely for sparing time for us and giving us an opportunity to discuss various issues and problems related to the study.

We are extremely grateful to Dr. Mulk Raj Anand for giving us an inspiring message for the present research study.

I owe a deep sense of gratitude to Dr. George Mathew, Director, Institute of Social Sciences, New Delhi who extended magnanimous guidance, help and cooperation in completing this project satisfactorily.

Dr. P.S.K. Menon, former consultant, Backward Classes Division of the Planning Commission, Government of India has been closely associated with me since the inception of the project. I would like to express my gratitude for his unflinching support in the completion of this study. I take this opportunity also to express my thanks to Shri Arun K. Ghosh for his valuable suggestions especially with regard to tabulation of data.

We also acknowledge our sincere thanks to all the members of the Institute of Social Sciences, particularly to Mr. Madhusudan Nair, Administrator, ISS, who graciously extended help and cooperation with all infrastructural support; to Ms. Molly Paul, who typed the manuscripts meticulously with sincere devotion; to Ms. Sapna Sharma for secretarial assistance and to Mr. Balwant Singh Rawat for all the logistic support.

March 31, 1996 BAKSHI D. SINHA
Advisor

Preface

(Revised and Enlarged Edition)

THE need for the second edition of Environmental Sanitation, Health and Panchayati Raj emerged out of the ever increasing demand for the book by many national and international organisations. Moreover, it was decided to have a quick appraisal of implementation and performance of different Models presented in the book.

In this context, we made an extensive search for appraisal of different models and to obtain secondary information through meetings and interviews with concerned Central and State Government officials, block, district and panchayat functionaries as well as international organisations and directly from the NGOs implementing these programmes.

It is most disheartening to note that inspite of visits and enquiries with the concerned implementing agencies, the secondary data and information were not forthcoming from many organisations. However, we were able to procure authentic data and information from some of the States viz., West Bengal, Rajasthan and Uttar Pradesh concerned with UNICEF assisted programmes; from Gujarat and Karnataka concerned with World Bank assisted programmes; from World Health Organisations; Pondicherry: Biovillage Model concerned with M.S. Swaminathan Research Foundation; and Orissa and Goa concerned with Sulabh International Social Service Organisations (SISSO). In addition we made critical appraisal of the implementation of the Models for which secondary data and information were available. It may be stated here that the implementation and performance of the Ram Krishna Mission known as Midnapore District Model in West Bengal; M.S. Swaminathan Research Foundation; Biovillage Model in Pondicherry; World Bank sponsored project Model in Gujarat and Karnataka; and

Sulabh International Social Service Organisation (SISSO) Models in Orissa and Goa concerned with water supply and sanitation deserve recognition as they are steadily progressing. But they have still to fully meet the aspirations of the local people to their satisfaction as organisational and institutions mechanism have still to reach to the door steps of the households through the Panchayati Raj system.

We have also reviewed the salient aspects of Rural Water Supply and Sanitation aspects as stated in the Eighth Plan document along the thrust objectives and priorities of the tentative Ninth Five Year Plan while bringing out the Revised and Enlarged Edition.

We are extremely grateful to all those, who provided us published and unpublished data and information and without their cooperation, it would not have been possible to bring out the Revised and Enlarged Edition.

We are also thankful to our publisher: Concept Publishing Company, New Delhi for their professional excellence in publishing the revised and enlarged edition on time.

We must convey our sincere gratitude to Dr. George Mathew, Director, Institute of Social Sciences, New Delhi, who provided support and encouragement to complete this task with patience and forbearance.

Our sincere and special gratitude is due to Dr. P.S.K. Menon, who has been closely associated with me in this project from its inception.

We also acknowledge our sincere thanks to all members of the Institute of Social Sciences, particularly Mr. Madhusudan Nair, Administrator, Ms. Molly Paul, who typed the manuscripts patiently with sincere devotion; Mr P.N. Kuttappan and Mr. Krishnan Namboodiri who did the layout of the book for publication; Ms. Sapna Sharma for secretarial assistance and to Mr. Balwant Singh Rawat and Mr. C. Gopi for all logistic support.

February 20, 1999

BAKSHI D. SINHA
Advisor
Institute of Social Sciences

CHAPTER - I

INTRODUCTION

IN considering environmental sanitation and health issues in Panchayati Raj set-up, the whole gamut of rural development would necessarily have to be examined, for the subject under study is an integral part of rural development. It is well known that rural development had been accorded a prominent place in the agenda during our national struggle for freedom under the benevolent leadership of Mahatma Gandhi. It is ironical that the plan era that followed independence, did not, however, assign the prominence that rural development deserved.

It is not necessary in a report of this kind to philosophize on the virtues of sanitation and health care. Sanitation is an exhaustive expression encompassing personal and domestic hygiene including disposal of human excreta, waste water and solid waste disposal, food hygiene and all other relevant components of a healthy living, which help in achieving environmental-friendly abode for the individual, the family, the community and the society as a whole. Thus, while sanitation is a comprehensive and wider desideratum aimed at efficient human resource development, efforts in our country have mostly been concentrated in constructing, at government cost a targeted number – far below the requirements – of sanitary latrines in a few selected areas leaving untouched and untapped the vast resources of people's initiatives in an institutionalised manner and ignoring the other requisite components, especially safe drinking water. It is no wonder, therefore, that the percentage of rural population covered by sanitary facilities (under the State and Central programmes) could reach only 2.8 per cent at the end of 1991-92 from 0.8 per cent at the beginning of 1987-88.

Five-Year Plan and Rural Development

It is unfortunate that it was only after the completion of four Five-Year Plans that a specific plan strategy with focus on rural population to tackle their minimum needs was evolved. Further, it was only in March 1995 that the Central government thought it appropriate to create new departments to focus greater attention on poor of rural and urban areas with reference to their basic needs. It was only during the Fifth Plan period that a comprehensive diagnosis of poverty scenario was made. The Fifth Plan approach document stated that, "the elimination of abject poverty will not be attained as a corollary to certain acceleration in the rate of growth of the economy alone". But, improvements in environmental sanitation and health have direct correlation with levels of living. Improvement in health care can be attained only when hunger and thirst are quenched and minimum shelter and clothing are provided for. Indeed, the maladies that afflict rural development including those in sanitation and health care spheres, are not materially different from those that perpetuate rural poverty. Notwithstanding appreciation of these general features and initiation of very many programmes, specific missions and special plans, the fact that much headway could not be made in tackling effectively the problems of rural development, will be borne by the assertions in the Eighth Plan document that, "the achievements have not been commensurate with resources spent on them . . . it is estimated that about one-third of them (beneficiaries) do not even have the original asset that was given to them".

Interestingly, the Eighth Five-Year Plan (1992-97) document notes that, "safe drinking water supply and basic sanitation are vital human needs for health and efficiency. Disease and death, particularly of children, every year and drudgery of women are directly attributable to lack of these essentials". Yet it is only, "envisaged to achieve coverage of about 5 per cent of rural population (cumulative) with their full involvement with sanitation facilities", by the end of the Eighth

Plan. Also, programmes to cover about 3000 'No Source' hardcore problem villages and about 1.5 lakh villages including hamlets, which were partially covered, are proposed to be fully covered with safe drinking water facilities on a sustainable basis in phases by the end of the Eighth Plan. The magnitude of the problems and the preparedness to tackle them are thus clear. At this pace, the desired goal of 'total sanitation and health care' for rural areas will be realised after a long period.

Administrative Structure for Implementation of Rural Sanitation Programmes

At this stage, it would be informative to furnish some details about administrative structure for implementation of these items. As per the Seventh Schedule to the Constitution, drinking water supply and sanitation are State subjects. At the Central level, the Ministry of Urban Development was the nodal agency for the sector till the beginning of the Seventh Five-Year Plan. Subsequently, the item "rural water supply and sanitation" was transferred to the Department of Rural Development. Rural water supply was an important constituent of the State Sector Minimum Needs Programme during the Seventh Plan period. In 1986, the National Drinking Water Mission, popularly known as the Technology Mission, was launched with a view to provide scientific and cost-effective impact to the Accelerated Water Supply Programme. In the same year (1986), it was also decided that a portion of the funds under the Rural Employment Programme and Indira Awas Yojana (housing scheme for members of the Scheduled Caste and Scheduled Tribe communities) could also be utilised for the rural sanitation. From 1987-88, rural sanitation programme was also added to the State Sector Minimum Needs Programme. In November 1986 a new Centrally-sponsored Rural Sanitation Programme (CRSP) was launched.

The guidelines for the Centrally-sponsored Rural Sanitation Programme were first issued in 1986. Based on the feedback received on implementation of the programme from the States, UNICEF and voluntary organisations, the programme was revised in March, 1991. The programme was further revised in June 1993 based, *inter alia*, on the recommendations of the

National Seminar on Rural Sanitation in September 1992 and the strategy outlined in the Eighth Five Year Plan. In her Foreword to the "General Guidelines for Implementation" of CRSP, Smt. Nirmala Buch, Secretary, Ministry of Rural Development (now Ministry of Rural Areas and Employment) stated that, "the revised programme aims at generation of felt need and people's participation." A salient feature of the revised programme is to develop at least one Model Village covering facilities like sanitary latrines, conversion of dry-latrines, garbage pits, soak pits, drainage, pavement of lanes, sanitary latrines in village institutions, cleanliness in ponds, tanks, clean surrounding around handpumps and other drinking water sources. The objectives of the CRSP were spelt out as:

(i) to accelerate coverage of rural population, especially among the households below poverty line with sanitation facilities, complementing the efforts in rural water supply and slowly breaking the vicious circle of disease, morbidity and poor health resulting from insanitary conditions and water-borne diseases;
(ii) to generate felt need through awareness creation and health education, involving voluntary organisations and Panchayati Raj Institutions, helping thereby to establish sanitary latrines with lesser dependence on government subsidy;
(iii) to eradicate manual scavenging by converting all existing dry latrines in rural areas into low-cost sanitary latrines; and
(iv) to encourage suitable cost-effective and appropriate technologies to support the other objectives.

The strategy for implementation of CRSP includes provision of appropriate level of subsidy, to encourage buying facilities through markets and sanitary marts, intensive campaign, establishment of sanitary complexes exclusively for women and encourage locally suitable and acceptable models of latrines.

Assessment

While it is premature to make a meaningful assessment of the revised Central Rural Sanitation Programme, the apprehension is that the programme is loaded with construction/conversion of latrines, with very little role for Panchayati Raj Institutions, some exceptions in one or two places. The crucial point is that the expected cumulative coverage of population under rural sanitation by the end of the Eighth Plan is only to be a mere five per cent as indicated in the Plan document. The relevant Table 1.1 is given below.

It has been officially recognised[1] that the concept of total environmental sanitation was absent, and that linkage of the programme with primary health care, water availability, removal of 'illiteracy' and women's welfare need attention. It is unfortunate that the sanitation programme should have been taken as a package of service rather than mere construction of latrines and that operation and maintenance of water supply and sanitation installations in the country is badly neglected. The Plan document also recognised[2] that the earlier efforts to discourage manual scavenging and liberate families engaged in the inhuman task had not borne satisfactory results. It was, therefore, suggested that the ongoing programmes for liberation and rehabilitation of scavengers should be streamlined to cover legislation, involvement of NGOs and adequate funding.

Eighth Plan Thrust and Strategies

The Eighth Five-Year Plan document of the Planning Commission explains[3] that, "based on the experience gained in the recent years and taking note of issues which have emerged, strategies and Plan thrusts have been evolved to cope with the challenges". Accordingly, it was suggested[4] that the Rural Sanitation Programme may be restructured providing for the four elements noted below:

(i) all activities under RSP will be undertaken through local body/village panchayat and with beneficiary participation;

TABLE 1.1

Physical Achievement Envisaged at the End of Eighth Plan

(Population in Million)

Sl. No.	Sub-Sector	Envisaged coverage as on 31.03.1992		Expected coverage during the Eighth Plan	Expected cumulative coverage at the end of the Eighth Plan	
		Population	Percentage@	Population*	Population	Percentage@
1	2	3	4	5	6	7
1.	Rural Sanitation	16.96	2.73	16.80	33.76	5.00
2.	Rural Water Supply	486.11	78.40	188.69	674.80	100.00

Note: @ Percentage is with respect to total projected rural population on the date.
* Including augmentation/improvement of services as appropriate.

Source: Eighth Five Year Plan, 1992-97, Vol. II, Government of India, Planning Commission, New Delhi.

(ii) wherever feasible, NGOs will be involved in implementation of the programme;
(iii) women will be actively associated with the implementation of the programme; and
(iv) some contribution should be solicited from the beneficiaries atleast in the form of physical labour, in order to engender among them the realisation that the assets created belong to the local community.

Eighth Plan: Rural Sanitation Programme (RSP)

On the basis of thrust and strategies suggested for the implementation of Rural Sanitation Programme stated above in this chapter, for the Eighth Plan, an outlay of Rs. 674 crore was made to cover an additional 2 to 3 per cent of the rural population. Meanwhile, during this plan period the demand for sanitary latrines increased from 11 per cent to 16 per cent because of growth of population. Hence, the expenditure on RSP also increased to about 55.5 per cent of the plan outlay as allocated to the central and State Governments, inclusive of IAY, JRY, UNICEF, CAPART and other NGOs financial contributions in Rural Sanitation Programmes.

The Thrust and Strategies were given credence, particularly to the people Below Poverty Level (BPL) for conversion and construction of sanitary latrines and secondly, interest-free loan was also provided to Private Entrepreneurs/Panchayats to establish sanitary marts in order to facilitate the people with sanitary materials. Moreover, NGOs and Voluntary Organisations were encouraged to organise the people through Panchayats and sensitise them to accept the sanitary package for construction of drains, soakage and garbage pits in their household as a measure to improve environmental sanitation and health care of each person in rural areas.

Water Supply

Eighth Plan outlay of Rs. 10,055 crores for Rural Water Supply Programme was to cover this facility to 100 per cent in rural areas from the estimated 78 per cent. In order to achieve this objective, the scheme of Accelerated Rural Water Supply Programme (ARWSP) was launched to cover all 'problem villages' along with those villages, which were either partially or wholly covered under this programme. The main aim was to ensure quality water in all villages along with infrastructure facilities and support services through management of human resources. Rajiv Gandhi National Drinking Water Mission was constituted to provide feedback for this task.

Eighth Plan review presented in the Draft Ninth Five Year Plan document Report (1997-2002, page 275) indicates "that the rural water supply programmes have covered 3.38 lakh villages/ habitations during the Eighth Plan". It is stated that "after the survey, 1.12 lakh villages Not Covered (NC), 1.50 lakh villages Partially Covered (PC) and 0.11 villages of Quality Problems (QP)", which were either wholly or partially, able to provide safe drinking water supply to about 85 per cent of the rural population of 1991 census. In other words about 6.10 lakh villages were provided access to this vital basic need for human existence. Nevertheless, the task of the Ninth Five Year Plan is still to cover all the 0.61 Not Covered (NC) villages, 3.79 Partially Covered (PC) villages and 1.51 Quality Problem (QP) villages. In other words, during Ninth Plan 5.91 lakh villages have still to be covered, wholly or partially, to make it possible for these facilities at the doorstep of each citizen.

Another initiative taken during Eighth Plan was to provide institutional mechanism through Panchayats for safe drinking water and sanitation schemes by people's participation in the process of planning and implementation of these schemes as envisaged in The Constitution (73rd Amendment Act). It suggests that the villagers have to be motivated not only for implementation of these schemes but also to accept the responsibility of repairs and maintenance of Water supply system and Sanitary facilities provided to them on the basis of Maharashtra and Midnapore Models. Each Panchayat will have to constitute a water committee and sanitation committee of trained people or caretaker (representing atleast two women) who may look after the operation and maintenance of the assets created for the village community. This process will be sustainable for these schemes.

Ninth Plan: Priorities and Strategies

The Ninth Plan sub-group of the Planning Commission on Environment and Health had concluded that "the unsatisfactory progress in safe drinking water supply and sanitary disposal of solid and liquid wastes contributed to the continued high morbidity from water-borne and vector-borne diseases" (Ninth Five Year Plan 1997-2002, page 278). The Expert Group, therefore, recommended that "water quality monitoring and surveillance" as well as solid waste management be given priority in order to reduce morbidity due to water and vector-borne diseases.

The universal coverage of safe drinking water supply in each village/habitation through different programmes has been one of the main strategies of the Ninth Plan. For this different norms of water supply lpcd for every person with minimum and maximum distance between 0.5 km and 1.6 km have been provided. The main thrust is that "water is perceived in the rural areas as a social good and is based on the principle of effective demand which should broadly correspond to the standard of service that the users are willing to maintain, operate and finance" the Fifth Plan document states. The Fifth Plan, therefore, suggests radical change in the management of water supply and its use, with complete people's participation under the Panchayati Raj Institutions. It encourages private sector initiatives for construction and maintenance of rural water supply and environmental sanitation and to replicate the Model of Sri Satya Sai Trust, Nilayam (Puttaparty), Andhra Pradesh in this regard.

The Draft Ninth Plan document admits that so far elimination of manual scavenging has not achieved the desired success in urban areas. Hence, it suggests demand-driven approach for construction of new-latrines and conversion of dry-latrines in rural areas and not the supply-driven approach. It advocates to accept the Midnapore Model with "little or no-subsidy or Government intervention" as a self-sustaining and self-financing scheme for not only construction or conversion also practically all rural environmental sanitation programme implemented in this model along with income generation activities for sustainability of this Rural Development Programme.

Studies

There are innumerable studies available both within and outside the country, where plans, programmes and strategies have been evaluated with reference to rural sanitation in general and specific components of RSP in particular, such as conversion of dry-latrines, role of NGOs, beneficiaries' involvement etc. It is not our intention to narrate in this study the results of such studies in any great detail. No doubt, appropriate references would be made in the text of the report wherever relevant. All the same an illustrative list of such studies conducted in the recent past is appended to this report in Annexure - I.

The one summary conclusion that can be drawn from these studies is that while we are *adept* and even exceedingly *apt* in evolving theoretical formulations and planning strategies, we lack sincerity and seriousness in implementation and enthusiasm and vigour in realising the full benefits of government-sponsored programmes.

The Present Study

This study oriented in the past has its focus on the future, to help usher in a new era of healthy 'Rural Sanitation Regime'. In this search for an affordable package of Environmental Sanitation and Health inputs, the assessment of existing models as well as possible interventions through people's initiatives both through the NGO network and Panchayati Raj structure would be made. The endeavour will not be to swell the literature with a study report but to offer workable alternatives to make rural people's life more comfortable.

REFERENCES

1. Eighth Five Year Plan, p.377.
2. p. 377, *ibid.*
3. p. 381, *ibid.*
4. p. 381, *ibid.*

CHAPTER - II

RURAL SANITATION AND HEALTH MODELS

APPROPRIATE sanitation and safe drinking water are basic facilities for health care strategy. They, therefore, constitute the most important factor of Health for All (HFA) strategy of our country. Contaminated drinking water and poor sanitation are the main causes of high mortality in our country (80/1000). Sanitation is a composite and comprehensive expression covering personal hygiene, domestic cleanliness, favourable environmental condition, safe disposal of human excreta, solid waste and waste water disposal. It is now recognised that lack of sanitation facilities is one of the factors adversely affecting the life of the people. It has also been officially accepted that, in development planning, rural sanitation did not receive the attention, it deserved for a long period. It is indeed a matter of great concern that large parts of our countryside are bereft of an appropriate sanitary design capable of obviating influences injurious to health. According to an estimate, about 0.17 million children are affected by poliomyelitis, 0.25 million die of tetanus and 1.5 million die of diarrhoea and dehydration every year. Although the programme for providing sanitation facilities gained only some momentum during the U.N. International Drinking Water Supply and Sanitation Decade (1981-91), its effect did gain sustainable long term impact. According to the latest available information, 0.1 per cent of our rural population had access to sanitation facilities in 1970; 0.5 per cent in 1980; 2.45 per cent in 1990, which it was expected to increase to about 2.73 per cent in 1992.

It is against this background that the present study has to be viewed. Also, the role of international organisations like UNICEF, World Bank, DANIDA and others in collaborating with India, as well as Indian NGOs with their avowed objectives of developing community-based approaches to the problem so as to be in conformity with the socio-economic and cultural diversity of the Indian population in the envisaged Panchayati Raj structure has to be appreciated.

To briefly recapitulate, the UNICEF took initiative in 1982 to collaborate with three NGOs in West Bengal. Later, five blocks in Orissa were taken up. Subsequently, the programme was extended to parts of Andhra Pradesh, Maharashtra, Madhya Pradesh, Gujarat, Tamil Nadu and Uttar Pradesh. It was in 1987 that the UNICEF collaboration with India, extended substantially in West Bengal, Tamil Nadu, Rajasthan and Uttar Pradesh to more areas, in the shape of what has now been called models.

The World Bank collaboration with India in the field of sanitation and water supply schemes was taken up in the eighties in Gujarat, and quite recently in Karnataka, Maharashtra and Uttar Pradesh.

Besides these, DANIDA, an Indo-Dutch collaboration for tackling the problems of sanitation and safe-drinking water in Karnataka, Kerala, Orissa and Tamil Nadu are noteworthy though not so significant considering the magnitude of the problem. A complete list of externally funded projects is given at Annexure - II. In the meantime, along with these efforts, the Planning Commission constituted the "Task Force on Self-Managed Institutions for Integrated Development" which submitted its Report in December 1991. It stated that, "the key to efficient utilization of resources lies in creation of appropriate self-managed organisation at all levels with a stress on people's participation as a key element in the process of development". While examining the existing institutional structures, the said Task Force realized that presently "Panchayat is no longer a social institution and is considered as an agent of the government." Consequently, wastage is high, convergence is low and the end product of development process is not visible". The Task Force, therefore, recommended strategies for changes in development administration by creating a new Institutional model called "Vikas Sangam" at different levels i.e. Apex or State level, District, Block, and Village levels. This is in consonance with three-tier Panchayati Raj structure as envisaged in 1992 Amendment Act. Further, the Task Force recommended "increasing the outlay on Voluntary Organisations having track records to achieve the multiplier effect of the process of development at the grassroots in the field of education, health, family planning, sanitation, energy, water and agriculture including social forestry and environment."

A. UNICEF ASSISTED PROGRAMMES

1. TAMIL NADU

Periyar Model

Periyar district in Tamil Nadu, named after renowned freedom fighter and social worker, E.V.R. Periyar, was carved out of Coimbatore district in 1979. The district, having a geographical area of 8209 sq. km and a population of 23.20 lakhs (1991 Census) is prosperous in agriculture. Major industries of textiles, sugar, animal feeds and foods are contributing to the growth of the district. The headquarters of the district, Erode, having a geographical area of 5089 sq. km. and a population of 2.32 lakhs is a famous 'texcity' the weekly textile shanty or major textile market, where traders from various parts of the country come regularly for business. For administrative purposes, the district is divided into three regions, namely, Erode, Gopichettipalayam and Dharapuram. There are, in the district, 7 talukas, 20 development blocks, 61 town panchayats and 510 revenue villages.

It is significant that the literacy rate of 53.80 in the district is a little higher as compared to the All India level of 52.21 per cent but is lower as compared to the State level literacy of 62.60 per cent (1991 Census). It is also significant to note that Periyar district has birth, death and infant mortality rates of 14.2,

6.3 and 40.0 per thousand respectively, which are far below the All India rates of 30.5, 10.2 and 91.0 per thousand respectively.

(1) The Periyar CDD-WATSAN (Control of Diarrhoeal Diseases-Water and Sanitation) project is implemented by the concerned governmental departments with financial assistance from UNICEF. This integrated approach to rural health care was introduced in Periyar district in the middle of 1991, where the Intensive Sanitation Programme was already taking roots, having been introduced in 1989. The programme benefits 97 villages of eight development blocks of the district, namely Sathyamangalam, Mulanur, Perundurai, Ammapettai, Anthiyur, T.N Palayam, Uthukuli and Vellakoil.

Based on the concept of Community Based Convergent Services (CBCS), the CDD-WATSAN programme has set the following targets:

(a) Reduce the incidence of diarrhoeal diseases among children under 5 years to 25 per cent by 1994.
(b) Provide universal access to safe-drinking water and improved sanitation coverage by 1995.

In regard to the operational details for control of diarrhoeal diseases, mention must be made of the facilities introduced in the "shape of District Diarrhoea Training Unit established in the District General Hospital at Erode, the headquarters of Periyar district. As to the details, when infants afflicted with diarrhoea symptoms are brought to the hospital, they are guided to the special paediatric ward, where children are administered ORS. Further, the mother is briefed on the availability and use of ORS at home to derive full benefits of the dose. Mothers are also instructed on the beneficial aspects of continuous feeding and increased availability of fluids at home during diarrhoea attack. In addition to the facility available at Erode, 18 "ORT corners" have been set up at different Primary Health Centres of the district to augment timely availability of ORS and render advice to mothers on the correct use of ORS and other home made fluids. To meet the demands of ORS at family level, ORS depots have been set up in all the 97 villages covered by the programme. At the grassroots level, the midday meal centre is organised by the Tamil Nadu Nutrition Project workers as also

CBCS leaders. They are also oriented towards managing ORT Depots.

In the 'sanitation' component of this particular programme, provision of subsidy for household Pour-Flush (P.F) latrines is made. The total cost of construction of a P.F. latrine has been worked out to be Rs 1,600 of which the beneficiary contributes Rs. 320 (20% of the total cost) UNICEF Rs. 400 (25% of the total cost) and the remaining Rs. 880 shared equally (Rs. 440 each) by the State and Central governments. It is reported that by the end of March 1994, the number of families who completed the P.F. latrines was 38,625. During 1994-95, it is reported that 5,000 more families will be covered under this programme.

Another feature of the sanitation programme is that of training local masons in construction of P.F. latrines. By May, 1994 about 100 persons had already been trained. Although, promotion of sanitary mart at each block headquarters has been taken up, yet the concept has not gained acceptance.

The project has the laudable objective of attaining school sanitation, which necessarily has the potential of spread effect in an effective manner. The provision of subsidy to 718 elementary schools out of 1200 as in May-June 1994 to construct P.F. latrines is a major achievement. The project authorities propose to develop two schools in each block "as a model school for sanitation and personal hygiene", which it is expected would lead to better demonstration effect resulting in innovative ventures at institutional levels.

Promotion of hand-washing with soap in all the 97 villages before cooking, eating, feeding/breast feeding and after defecation or disposal of child's stool etc. are extensively propagated through appropriate modes of dissemination.

Constant contact by motivators at grassroots level covering every section of population through appropriate communication campaign ensure people's participation in a useful manner. Even wall paintings to convey the 'messages' are undertaken.

Village Level Operation and Maintenance (VLOM)

For the operation, T. N. Palayam Development Block having CDD-WATSAN component under implementation was selected.

The programme was to convert 145 Mark II pumps into Mark III at a total cost of about Rs. 30 lakhs. The sharing of the cost was worked out as: (i) UNICEF, Rs. 15.40 lakhs; (ii) State government: Rs. 7.30 lakhs; and (iii) panchayat Rs. 7.30 lakhs.

Having involved the existing women groups and interested villagers, 24 WATSAN committees were established and 48 village mechanics and 148 motivators were trained. This core-group would sensitise the whole village population towards achieving the village level operation and maintenance concept in an effective and coordinated manner.

The involvement of panchayats in the village sanitation committee of users in respect of Water Sanitation (WATSAN) is noteworthy. Each village committee will have 7-9 motivated members including panchayat President and one or two panchayat members. Another feature is that each WATSAN Committee would have about 4 or more women members. A two-day orientation camp is organised by the District Administration to familiarise the committee members with different aspects, including hand pump maintenance. An even more significant aspect is that the resource persons for the camps are drawn from local NGOs.

Development of Women and Children in Rural Areas (DWACRA)

Since the introduction of the scheme in the district in 1983 and upto May 1994, a total of 705 women's groups were formed through which 10,547 women beneficiaries took advantage of the designated programmes. The impressive range of 85 trades include traditional items like pottery and handloom weaving to chemical-based activities and synthetic gem cutting. In order to tackle marketing problems, a District Supply and Marketing Society (DSMS) with membership of about 400 DWACRA groups has been set up. Initially, MYRADA would assist in the operations, which would ultimately pass on to DSMS. A proposal for assistance by the Government/UNICEF to the venture was considered at one stage.

Community Based Convergence Services (CBCS)

On an experimental basis, the services were introduced in three blocks viz., Sathyamangalam, Perundurai and Mulanur in late 1991. As a matter of fact, the introduction of the concept in 1991 facilitated easy launching of CDD-WATSAN in the above blocks. Appropriate committees with women representation were formed at District, Block and village levels. MYRADA conducted training for the members of the committees. Ultimately, it was possible to list out the "expectations" and demands from the villagers such as Pour-Flush latrines, pipelines, roads, lights, buildings, bus stops etc., which the District Administration was unable to finance. Thus, through an awareness, prioritisation and focussing of problems, assessing field realities was possible.

Conclusion

The Periyar district project in Tamil Nadu has adopted the concept of " cleanliness" with household P.F. latrines as the entry point. This Model provides an illustration to establish that the prevalent government infrastructure could be effectively utilised through proper planning, leadership and motivation. The entire project is run through well-organised and motivated government functionaries with minimum support from NGOs and involvement of panchayats.

2. WEST BENGAL

Midnapore Model

Midnapore, originally called Medinipore, is one of the prosperous districts of West Bengal. Pandit Ishwar Chandra Vidyasagar, who hailed from Birsingha village of this district led socio-cultural reforms through education and literacy campaigns, which uprooted many social evils in India. The aura of Vidyasagar is vibrant even now in the psyche of the people for accepting social change. This is substantiated by the fact that Midnapore district has been recognised as a total literate district due to mass literacy campaign. In 1991 Census the level of literacy rate was recorded as 69.32 per cent, which is reasonably above the All-India level of 52.21 per cent and that of West Bengal level of 57.70 per cent. Male literacy (81.27%) and female literacy (56.63%) are also high as compared to All-India and State rates.

The total population of the district was recorded as 83.32 lakhs in 1991 Census, which represented an increase of 23.6 per cent over 1981 Census population of 67.43 lakhs. It is significant that the urban population of 8.21 lakhs denote an increase by 43.3 per cent in 1991 Census, i.e. from 5.73 lakhs in 1981 Census. But the rural population of 75.11 lakhs in 1991 Census, as compared to 61.70 lakhs in 1981 Census, represented an increase of 21.7 per cent. It indicates that urbanisation is taking its roots in Midnapore district.

It is an agriculturally prosperous district, where majority of the people consume rice. Major industrial establishments viz., Hindustan Levers Ltd., Indian Rayon Industry Ltd., HIM Containers Ltd., Burn Standard Ltd., and Universal Paper Mills Ltd. are operating and provide employment to the people of the district.

For administrative purposes, there are 7 sub-divisions consisting of 54 Community Development Blocks covering 14,081 sq. kms.

Intensive Sanitation Project

The Intensive Sanitation Project (ISP) was formulated and initiated in the above social, physical and administrative structure in collaboration with the Government of India, West Bengal State Government and UNICEF during October 1989. The Ramakrishna Mission Loksiksha Parishad (RKMLP – henceforth the Mission) Narendrapur, a dedicated Voluntary Organisation was selected to implement the project. The Mission started implementation of the project in April 1990 with a target to complete it by March 1995.

Objectives

The main objectives of the project are: (a) to make people aware of the personal and community hygiene through sanitation, education and motivation for acceptance of different health and sanitation programmes; (b) to reduce infant mortality rate; (c) to reduce water-borne diseases through improved sanitation facilities; (d) to provide a package of sanitation facilities such as low-cost latrines affordable to different economic categories of people as well as smokeless chulah, soak-pit and garbage-pit in households and institutions; (e) to install Tara Handpumps for providing safe drinking water; and (f) to establish inter-sectoral linkages for promoting income-generation activities, particularly amongst women.

Methodology and Strategy

The Mission developed a methodology and different operational strategies to achieve the main objectives for making sanitation programmes self-sustaining and self-expanding in the years to come.

The Main Operational Strategies are: (a) to provide Information, Education and Communication (IEC) for creating awareness amongst the rural people through trained volunteers, motivators and masons, who could work together along with already existing youth clubs at the village, block and district levels for implementing delivery system of the project; (b) to develop economically affordable low-cost models of latrines and other sanitary facilities as a Self-Financing Scheme acceptable to the beneficiaries; (c) to advocate to the members of the Panchayat Samiti and Government officials about the benefits of Self-Financing Approach and Social Mobilization Scheme.

Targets

The Mission set the main target of the project to cover: (a) 80 per cent of population by general advocacy of sanitation programme; (b) 75 per cent of the household through the package of sanitary facilities; and (c) 50 per cent of the household with actual construction of sanitary latrines and its use and maintenance.

Achievements

The main achievements of the ISP Midnapore Project from March 1990 to December 1993 has been on advocacy and development of infrastructure.

1. With regard to advocacy of sanitation concept, the Project involved village-level youth clubs at the grassroots and cluster organisations (consortium of clubs in the ISP at village or block level). It is reported that eleven cluster organisations has been developed with a network of 792 village youth clubs in 45 Blocks (out of 54 Blocks) in the district. For operational purposes, motivators are identified at the village club level. One motivator, works for 200 households at regular intervals, after getting training for two and a half days. It is significant to note that by the end of December 1993 i.e. within a period of three and a half years, training was imparted to 2016 village motivators, 1784 youth club leaders, 798 village masons, 604 smokeless-chullah workers, 669 Tara hand pump women caretakers and 896 water committee members. Besides, masons (32), drilling mistries (41), sanitary song singers (22), and field level project personnel (82) were also trained during this period. The ISP project has also given orientation training to about 5000 panchayat members and block level personnel in order to spread the messages of sanitation and social mobilisation activities through audio-visual materials.
2. It is indicated in the Progress Report (of RKMLP – Intensive Sanitation Project) that about 5 lakh low cost household latrines will be required to be installed to cover 50 per cent of the population of the district by the end of the century. It is also stated that the project has installed 37,288 units of low-cost household latrines between 1990 to 1993, and is expected to instal another 62,712 units (out of the estimated target of one lakh units) by 1995.

It may be noted that the project has designed twelve models of different specifications/cost of low cost household latrines. The unit cost of construction ranges from Rs. 230 to Rs. 3030.

Out of 37,288 units of household latrines installed between 1990 and 1993, the details of 26,305 units were processed and are given in Table 2.1:

TABLE 2.1
The Unit Cost of Construction Ranges

Sl. No.	Description of Latrine	Model	Cost Rs.	No.	Percent
1.	Direct One Pit (Non Lining Pit)	K	230	16222	61.67
2.	-do-	L	270		
3.	Direct One Pit (Lining with bricks/RCC Ring)	I	550	3577	13.60
4.	-do-	J	750		
5.	One Pit (Upto Plinth and Provision for 2nd Pit)	G	1050	892	3.39
6.	-do-	H	1350		
7.	One Pit (with brick superstructure and provision for 2nd Pit)	E	2150	274	1.04
8.	-do-	F	2350		
9.	Two Pit without superstructure	C	1450	1434	5.45
10.	-do- with superstructure	D	1750		
11.	Two Pit with brick superstructure	A	2550	3906	14.85
12.	-do-	B	3030		
	Total			26305	100.00

Source: Progress Report — 1993: Intensive Sanitation Project, Midnapore Ramakrishna Mission Lokshiksha Parishad, Narendrapur, West Bengal, p. 16, 1993.

It may be seen from Table 2.1 that 79.70 per cent of the household latrines were of One-Pit models and 20.30 per cent of Two-Pits (with or without superstructure). Maximum number of 16,222 units (61.67%) were of K and L models, followed by other models of One-Pit household latrines.

During our field visit, we discussed with some of the beneficiaries of One-Pit models to ascertain the effectiveness of these models. It was reported that most of the One-Pit latrines are filled-in with water and soil during rainy season or floods. Hence, they seek alternative avenues for defecation after rainy season or when flood is over. Some of the beneficiaries of K and L models stated that after monsoon or flood is over, they dig a pit somewhere nearby and put the RCC platform on top of it and then use it for defecation.

The question of sustainability of One-Pit latrine models thus becomes crucial as these do not resolve the problems of environmental pollution in rural areas. Besides, the entire cost incurred by beneficiaries of low income groups, becomes infructuous.

UNICEF Financial Support

It is reported that UNICEF financial support has been to the tune of Rs. 25 lakhs per annum for a period of about six years, which accounts for Rs. 1.50 crores. Besides, UNICEF also contributed Rs. 2 crores as a Revolving Fund for operation of the project. In other words, the total financial support has been to the extent of Rs. 3.50 crores only.

Revised Programme of Action (RPA)

The Revised Programmes of Action (POA) of the project in 1994 and 1995, on the basis of past experience of about three years, have listed out some achievements. They are as follows:

(a) It is reported that the target to cover 80 per cent of population of the district under general advocacy by 1995 has been achieved to the extent of 35 per cent population by middle of 1994 and the rest 45 per cent population is expected to be covered by 1995.

(b) Secondly, the project has already formed 11 cluster organisations with a network of 792 village youth clubs in 45 blocks of the district by middle of 1994 and the rest 9 cluster organisations (out of 20 cluster organisations) are expected to be established in the rest 9 blocks of the district by 1995. In other words, it is contemplated that 20 cluster organisations along with 1200 associated village youth clubs in all the 54 blocks will be achieved by 1995. It is further stated that one youth club will contact about 1000 to 1500 families (i.e. one motivator for 150 to 200 families) per cluster and work for advocacy, promotion, training, construction, and monitoring of the programme.

(c) Thirdly, there has been some significant changes in the operational strategy as stated in the Programme of Action (POA) of 1994 and 1995 in order to achieve the objectives and targets of the project. They are as follows:

(i) loan facilities would be available to very poor income group families in the lowest cost models of latrines (Rs. 230 and Rs. 270).

(ii) Cost of administration, training and advocacy would be recovered as service charge partially from unit cost of various sanitary facilities provided to the beneficiaries and the rest would be mobilized from government departments after 1995, when UNICEF withdraws financial support to the project.

(iii) After 1995, the implementation of the sanitation project would be taken up by local panchayats under the supervision of its various committees such as CDD-WATSAN at the grassroots and review committees at the district and State levels at regular intervals for smooth implementation and monitoring of the project.

(iv) One of the strategies of the Midnapore Model is the Social Marketing approach of Sanitation Development Programmes by setting up Sanitary Mart in each cluster. Thus, in Midnapore district each of the 20 cluster organizations will set up one Sanitary Mart in each cluster. This has been an accepted policy of the Government of West Bengal to be followed in all the 19 districts of the State. Initially, the emphasis was on the installation of low cost latrines. But now the project intends to provide other sanitary facilities such as smokeless chulhas, bathing platform, soak-pit, garbage pit besides sanitary latrines as a package through Self-Financing Approach in a cluster.

(v) Recently the Project authorities have submitted a proposal to introduce CDD-WATSAN strategy in order to control diarrhoeal diseases through the intervention of Diarrhoeal Management with ORS and safe-water supply programme (by installing Tara Hand Pumps) with the support from UNICEF.

The Revised Programme of Action (RPA) in 1995, after withdrawal of UNICEF financial support led to many changes in operational implementation strategy of sanitation and health programmes of the Mission in Midnapore district.

The progress Report of the Intensive Sanitation Project (ISP) states that the concept of training and advocacy, since inception of the programme in April 1990 till 1996 made salutary effect on cluster organisations at grassroot levels for achievements in various activities of the programme in many villages of different community development blocks. In other words, from April 1990 till April 1996, it is reported that 19 types of Training Courses were conducted in which 25,784 persons were trained having 726 number of courses in 14 cluster organizations.

With regard to Advocacy Programme (such as motivation camp, exhibition, wall-writing, video and slide show, home visit, songs squad programme and group meeting). Since inception upto December 1996 it is reported that the number of activities organized were 6,29,038 in which about 10.86 lakhs people participated.

The sanitation facilities created since inception till December 1996 includes: the number of Household Low Cost

Latrine HHLCL (1,32,950) constituting 65,935 Self-Finance Scheme – SFS (49.6%) and 67,016 Central Rural Sanitation Programme – CRSP (50.4%). It is estimated that in Self-Financing Scheme 52,144 (or 80%) are of one pit latrine. Besides HHLCL the other sanitation facilities provided during this period consists of Soakage Pit (409), Garbage Pit (4986), Bathing Platform (518), Washing Platform (182), Improved Chulha (12,775), Tara Hand Pump (546), Biogas link HHLCL (369) and O.R.S Packet Sold (48,446).

As stated earlier, there are 54 Community Development Blocks in Midnapore district, having 14 cluster organisations in which 1107 youth clubs have been constituted which are operating in 7,985 villages. It is to be noted that three sanitation Gram Panchayats have effectively advocated the Intensive Sanitation Programme (ISP) in 143 villages.

Conclusion

(a) Midnapore Intensive Sanitation Programme has yet to be thoroughly investigated as it has not achieved three notable targets according to time frame of the project as discussed earlier in this section of the study viz., (a) general advocacy of sanitation programme, (b) package of sanitary facilities and (c) construction of Household Low Cost Sanitary latrines and its use and maintenance. So far, it has not been investigated whether One-Pit latrine of different models under Self-Financing Scheme are still in use and has not been a waste. This is a crucial question which calls for an enquiry to determine the efficacy of these models as designed in this project. If found faulty, it may cause serious problems of environmental pollution in many villages of the district.

(b) The State government on August 14, 1997 gave administrative powers to Panchayats. It has allowed 29 departments to work, plan and execute projects such as power, irrigation, roads, education, health etc. and about 50% of plan funds have been allocated to be spent by Panchayats under the guidance and control of the District Planning Coordination Council (DPCC) which has been revived. Out of 50% allocation, 30% will be utilised through Zilla Parishads and 20% through Panchayat Samities.

(c) Besides above developments in the activities of the Panchayats, it is reported that the "West Bengal government has announced that all Non-Government Organizations which have been receiving foreign funding and/or government aid will from now on have to execute their rural development and social welfare works under direct control of the Panchayats". Under this arrangement, it has to be ascertained as to what extent the Mission, which implemented ISP Midnapur Model has been able to effectively execute the project in the Panchayats.

Ramakrishna Mission Loksiksha Parishad, Narendrapur (Source: *Gramseva*, 1999, pp. 26-28) states the impact of the whole programme in Midnapore district as follows:

1. The project has been able to saturate all the families with low cost latrines in 5 Gram panchayats in 238 villages and 85 per cent families in Tamluk II and Ramnagore II blocks. From this examples other 80 Gram panchayats and 10 Panchayat Samiti authorities came forward to install low cost latrine in all houses in their areas by end of 1999.
2. The Project is encouraging because a number of new village clubs in the Project district is coming forward to implement the Sanitation Project in their own areas. There has been a visible multiplier effect so far as the people's acceptance of the Project is concerned.
3. The common people including the low income groups and backward communities are coming forward to install the facilities.
4. Women groups are getting involved in motivating the menfolk to accept the facilities. This has enhanced the pace of growth of the movement.
5. The village level Panchayats are getting involved in the total process and advocating the idea regularly.
6. The District Administration and Panchayats are extending full help and cooperation in implementing the Project at all levels.
7. The Project has been able to create a sense of self-respect

amongst the womenfolk by giving importance to the housewives in decision making process for installation of household low cost latrine, smokeless chullahs etc.

8. The Project has been able to create a confidence amongst the village womenfolk by giving them the entire responsibility of repairing and maintenance of Hand Pumps.
9. The State Government has accepted the Medinipur model for all the districts of West Bengal. For wider coverage the Government has reduced the subsidy for beneficiaries under the centrally sponsored scheme of CRSP from Rs. 2,000 to Rs.200 for target families.
10. A number of State Governments have introduced self-financed sanitary projects in their areas and substantially reduced the quantum of subsidy. Many of them have also started involving village organisations in implementation of this programme.
11. The villages where more than 80 per cent households have adopted the low cost latrine and other facilities, impact on health has been very significant.
12. Social tension and conflict in many villages have come down because of social mobilisation through introduction of low cost latrine.
13. A new partnership has gown between Panchayat and voluntary social organisations through the project.

3. RAJASTHAN

Alwar Model

The Rural Sanitation Programme (RSP) was initiated by the Department of Rural Development and Panchayati Raj, Government of Rajasthan in collaboration with UNICEF in Alwar District in order to evolve a model. Later on, the programme was extended to Jaipur, Bhilwara, Tonk, Sawai Madhopur and Ajmer districts. In these six districts, 320 villages of 41 blocks were selected. Besides, the programme was also implemented in four districts with substantial tribal population viz., Banswara, Dungarpur, Udaipur and Rajsamand with the support of SWACH (a unit supported by UNICEF and SIDA). In 1992-93, sanitation programme was taken up in four more districts viz., Jhalawar, Nagaur, Jodhpur and Barmer under the Rajasthan Integrated Guineaworm Eradication Project (RIGEP). Later, two blocks (Rajgarh and Kishangarhbas) of Alwar district were also taken up under the Control of Diarrhoeal Diseases and Water and Sanitation Project (CDD-WATSAN Project).

It may be noted that the Rural Sanitation Programme was implemented in Rajasthan on the basis of the experience of Alwar Model.

Before explaining the Model, we would briefly discuss the demographic and salient features of the district.

The total population of the district was 17.71 lakhs in 1981 which increased to 22.97 lakhs in 1991 i.e. an increase of 29.70 per cent. The total area of the district is 8,380 sq. km. divided into 4 sub-divisions having 1892 villages in 14 blocks. Each block is having public health centres. The district educational facilities include of about 15,000 primary schools, 380 middle schools, 127 secondary schools and 17 senior secondary schools. The district literacy rate of 43.09 per cent is higher than the State literary rate of 38.55 per cent, but lower than the all-India average literacy rate of 52.21 per cent in 1991. Male literacy rate of 60.98 per cent is far above the female literacy rate of 22.54 per cent (1991 Census). The district is having major mineral products like copper, barium, sulphate, steatite, feldspar etc. The major industries are those of synthetic, syntex, chemicals and shaving products. Alwar town is a satellite town of the National Capital Region and is easily accessible from Delhi. The district has tourism prospects with many natural and historical locations.

With this background, Alwar district was selected by the Government of Rajasthan in collaboration with UNICEF to evolve a model for implementation of Rural Sanitation Programme. Initially, 102 villages were selected from 14 blocks of the district.

Objectives

The main objectives of RSP are:

(a) to provide a package of sanitary facilities such as sanitary latrines, soak-pits, washing and bathing platforms, garbage pits and improved chulhas at the household level as well as institutional/community levels and soak-pits with washing/bathing platform at public stand/handpump sites; and

(b) to create awareness through social mobilization activities with regard to health and sanitation education by involving voluntary organisations viz., Bharat Scouts and Guides as well as teachers and school children, particularly women of the village community.

In order to achieve the objectives, two Village Sanitation Motivators (VSM), one male and one female – are selected from each village. These motivators are initially imparted training for creating awareness about health and sanitation package programme. Subsequently, they motivate the village community with the help of IEC materials such as video-cassettes and posters at important places. At regular intervals, these motivators undergo refresher courses. In other words, the motivators are supposed to create demand for the package of sanitation facilities by beneficiaries and get those constructed at the household and community levels. An honorarium of Rs. 50 per month is paid to each VSM. Quarterly meetings are held at block level to review and sort out their problems, if any. Besides, awareness camp is also organised in each village once a year through the help of voluntary organizations like Bharat Scouts and Guides and National Cadet Corps (NCC).

Organisational and Management Structure

Sanitation Cell at the State level under the Department of Rural Development and Panchayati Raj, is the nodal agency for implementation and monitoring of the sanitation programme. The programme is implemented through the concerned officials at the district, block and village levels, with cooperation and participation of departments like, medical and health, PHED, education, women and child etc. UNICEF extended administrative and financial support not only in designing and giving a shape to the Alwar Model but also promoting sanitation programmes in other districts of Rajasthan.

Target

It is significant that the Rural Sanitation Programme has been proposed to be implemented in all the 30 districts of the State, out of which 17 districts are covered by UNICEF assistance. In order to achieve the objectives of the programme, Government of Rajasthan, set a target to provide sanitary facilities to atleast 25 per cent families by the turn of the century. Accordingly, it was proposed to implement installation of sanitary facilities at domestic and community/institutional levels during the financial year 1994-95 in all 30 districts of Rajasthan as follows:

		(No.)
(i)	Household latrines with sanitary package to families above poverty line	2,70,000
(ii)	Household latrines with sanitary package to families below poverty line	27,340
(iii)	Institutional latrines with sanitary facilities	490
(iv)	Construction of Facility Park for Women	25
(v)	Soak-pits/bathing platform near Public Stand Pump/Handpump Stand	990
(vi)	Training Centre	295
(vii)	Social Mobilization and Awareness-Building Camps	305

Financial Assistance Pattern

To attain the above targets a financial assistance pattern has been worked out, the cost being shared by the State government, Central government, UNICEF and also by beneficiaries/village community. The break-up of financial assistance/contribution pattern and the budget provisions made (cumulative) for the years 1993-94 and 1994-95 have been given in the following Table 2.2.

It can be seen from the Tables 2.2 and 2.3 that the financial contribution of the State and Central governments for construction of sanitary latrines is comparatively high 41.79%) as compared to UNICEF (16.42%). Practically in all sanitary facilities and other activities under the programme, the financial support of UNICEF ranges from 42.10 per cent in Facility Park for Women to 83.84 per cent in construction of sanitary facilities near PSP's and HPS's site as compared to State and Central government's share ranging from 28.95 per cent to 8.08 per cent each, respectively. Besides, the financial contribution of UNICEF for executing the programme in other sanitary packages as well as in training different levels of people for creating awareness through social mobilization activities, with organisational and administrative support, is higher.

As discussed earlier in this study, the main objective of Rural Sanitation Programme (RSP) has been to provide a package of sanitary facilities by creating awareness among the rural community with regard to sanitation and health education (particularly among the people living below poverty level-BPL).

The Progress Report of the Department of Rural Development and Panchayati Raj of Rajasthan, 1996-97 states that the Rural Sanitation Programme (RSP) was implemented in all the 31 districts in which 14 districts were allocated to the UNICEF for exclusive operations and in the rest 17 districts both the State and the Central governments contributed their financial share. It further states that it was proposed to provide 3,00,000 units/package of sanitary facilities to Non-Below Poverty Level families during 1994-95 and 1995-96. But, the achievement was only 90,527 Non BPL families in 1994-95 and 1,28,987 Non-BPL families in 1995-96. Nevertheless, the achievement made with regard to sanitary facilities provided to Below Poverty Level (BPL) families (who earn annual income of Rs. 11,000 only) has been quite impressive from 1991-92 to 1996-97, as shown in the Table 2.2 below.

TABLE 2.2

Sanitary Facilities provided to BPL Families 1991-92 to 1996-97

Year	Target	Achievement	Percentage
1991-92	12800	9441	73.70
1992-93	12733	12430	97.60
1993-94	12370	9558	77.26
1994-95	27340	21744	79.53
1995-96	20745	18456	89.00
1996-97	16500	9510	57.64
(As on January 1997)			

It may be noted that in Rajasthan there has been Sustainable Development in Rural Sanitation Programme because the Departments of Rural Development and Panchayati Raj with the support from the UNICEF and the Central government are implementing the RSP schemes of providing sanitary packages to the complete satisfaction of the beneficiaries. Rural sanitary marts in each panchayat samiti and facility parks for women as community complexes are not only acceptable to the village community but has improved their health and living standard to a great extent.

Besides, RSP sanitary facilities, the Panchayats have taken full responsibility to supervise implementation and operation, in providing low cost housing facilities and low cost land to the people of BPL.

The performance in RSP sanitary facilities provided in 14 districts where UNICEF has been implementing the programme is given in Table 2.5.

Conclusion

The programme is to be implemented in all the 30 districts, out of which UNICEF is operating in 17 districts. It is significant that it was the 'Alwar model' which effectively sensitised the planning process and implementation strategy in other districts of Rajasthan. Also, some innovative changes have been made over the years as reflected in the Guidelines of the Programme of Action (POA), such as:

(a) to establish 'Rural Sanitary Mart' in each Panchayat Samiti, for which Rs. 50,000 is provided. Besides, an amount of Rs. 18,000 is given as revolving fund for administrative purposes for two years. Further, Rs.12,000 is also paid for promoting and advocating the usefulness of the mart. These are all done with complete financial support of UNICEF;

TABLE 2.3
Financial Assistance Pattern

(In Rupees)

Sl. No.	Sanitary facilities	UNICEF Sponsored Districts					Other Districts			
		Financial Contribution					Financial Contribution			
		Total unit cost	State Govt.	Central Govt.	UNICEF	Benefi-ciary & community share	State Govt.	Central Govt.	UNICEF	Beneficiary & community share
1	2	3	4	5	6	7	8	9	10	11
(A)	Household Sanitary Package Facilities									
1.	Latrine	2,500	775	775	450	500	1,100	1,100		500
2.	Soak-pit	250			125	125	62.50	62.50		125
3.	Bathing/Washing Platform	250			125	125	62.50	62.50		125
(B)	Facility Park for Women	3,30,000	74,700	74,700	1,08,600	72,000	74,700	74,700	1,08,600	72,000

(Contd.)

TABLE 2.3 *(Contd.)*

1	2	3	4	5	6	7	8	9	10	11
(C)	Institutional Latrines-cum-Urinals	4,000			2,000	2,000	1,000	1,000		2,000
(D)	Soak-pits/ bathing plat-form near PSP's HP's, cattle pot, drainage con-struction	2,000			1,500	500	750	750		1,500

Source: Guidelines to Rural Sanitation Programme in Rajasthan, Department of Rural Development and Panchayati Raj, Jaipur, p. 11, 1994-95.

Notes:

1. Both the State and Central governments including UNICEF are concerned with construction of sanitary facilities at domestic and community levels as well as 'Facility Park for Women'.
2. The construction of 'Facility Park for Women' is for 48 families, and each family is provided one latrine and a bathroom in this complex.
3. The financial support for construction of institutional latrines-cum-urinals are contributed by different agencies stated above, but in case more funds are required in completing the construction of this sanitary facility, the Panchayat Samiti of the concerned village/area has to procure funds with people's cooperation or through education tax.

TABLE 2.4
Rural Sanitation Programme in Rajasthan
Budget Provision in 30 Districts (Cumulative)
(1993-94 and 1994-95)

(Rupees)

Sr. No.	Financial Assistance to Sanitary Facilities & Other Activities	Contribution from			
		State Govt.	Central Govt.	UNICEF	Total
1	2	3	4	5	6
1.	Latrines	2,28,53,500 (41.79)	2,28,53,500 (41.79)	89,73,000 (16.42)	5,46,80,000 (100.00)
2.	Other Sanitary Package	9,25,000 (13.94)	9,25,000 (13.94)	47,85,000 (72.12)	66,35,000 (100.00)
3.	Organisational Support	1,60,000 (16.33)	1,60,000 (16.33)	6,60,000 (67.34)	9,80,000 (100.00)
4.	PSP's/HPS's site facilities *	1,20,000 (8.08)	1,20,000 (8.08)	12,45,000 (83.84)	14,85,000 (100.00)
5.	Facility Park for women	18,67,500 (28.95)	18,67,500 (28.95)	27,15,000 (42.10)	64,50,000 (100.00)

(Contd.)

TABLE 2.4 *Contd.)*

1	2	3	4	5	6
6.	Training	10,35,850 (23.96)	10,35,850 (23.96)	22,50,800 (52.08)	43,22,500 (100.00)
7.	Social Mobilization	7,64,500 (16.75)	7,64,500 (16.75)	30,35,600 (66.50)	45,64,600 (100.00)
8.	Administration expenses	1,44,000 (24.49)	1,44,000 (24.49)	3,00,000 (51.02)	5,88,000 (100.00)
9.	Sanitary Mart	Nil	Nil	6,40,000 (100.00)	6,44,000 (100.00)
	Total	2,78,70,350 (34.69)	2,78,70,350 (34.69)	2,46,04,400 (30.62)	8,03,45,100 (100.00)

Source: Guidelines for Rural Sanitation Programme in Rajasthan, Department of Rural Development and Panchayati Raj, Jaipur, pp. 18 to 25, 1994-95.

* PSP = Public Stand Pump
HPS = Handpump Stand

TABLE 2.5
Performance of RSP Sanitary Facilities provided in 14 Districts by UNICEF Assistance

Sr. No	District	H/H Units	H/H soakage pit	Bathing platform	Instt. latrine	Hand pump sites	Total (3+4+5+6+7)	Advance Amount	Amount Pending (9-8)	Reimbursement Reimb (8-9)	Reimbursement Release	Reimbursement Balance to be released (11-12)
1	2	3	4	5	6	7	8	9	10	11	12	13
1.	Ajmer	112500	29625	31250	50000	60000	283375	448000	164625	NA	NA	NA
2.	Alwar	540000	137500	139625	36000	49500	902625	672000	-	230625	-	230625
3.	Banswara	284850	79125	79125	10000	39000	492100	448000	-	44100	-	44100
4.	Bhilwara	233550 123750	31250 10625	39000 15875	16000 2000	24000 1500	343800 153750	280000	-	217550	-	217550
5.	Dungarpur	270000	75000	75000	16000	18000	454000	224000	-	230000	-	230000
6.	Jaipur	360000	84750	96625	32000	61500	634875	336000	-	298875	-	298875
7.	Rajsamand	150750	36375	41875	18000	46500	293500	140000	-	153500	-	153500
8.	S. Madhopur	150750	41875	41875	4000	-	238500	224000	-	14500	-	14500

TABLE 2.5 (*Contd.*)

1	2	3	4	5	6	7	8	9	10	11	12	13
9.	Tonk	137250	23750	31375	2000	-	194375	168000	-	26375	-	26375
10.	Udaipur	145350	38625	39375	-	12000	235350	224000	-	14500	-	14500
11.	Barmer	157500	32125	32125	20000	-	241750	196000	-	45750	-	45750
12.	Jodhpur	18900 94050	5250 26125	5250 26125	-	-	29400 146300	252000	76300	-	-	-
13.	Jhalawar	-	-	-	-	-	-	140000	140000	-	-	-
14.	Nagour	197100 28800	54750 8000	54750 8000	6000 22000	6000 7500	318600 74300	168000	-	224900	-	224900
	Total	661950	158375	164375	40000	39000	1063700	-	-	-	-	-
	Total I & II	3005100	714750	757250	234000	325500	5036600	-	-	-	-	-
	Gr. Total	3005100	714750	757250	234000	325500	5036600	3920000	380925	1497525	-	1497525

Source: Additional Chief Town Planner, Department of Rural Sanitation, Jaipur.

(b) to construct "Facility Park for Women" as a community complex for 48 families, where each family is provided with a latrine and a bathroom. In this effort, the total unit cost of the complex has been estimated to be Rs. 3,30,000 in which percentage share of the financial contribution of the State government, Central government and UNICEF is 22.64, 22.64 and 32.91 per cent, respectively. Besides the beneficiary share of 21.81 per cent is quite significant;

(c) to impart effective training and orientation for various categories of people at different levels (i.e. State, district, block and village), it is proposed in the POA to establish 295 Training Centres in the State;

(d) to seek help and cooperation from Voluntary Organisations such as Bharat Scouts and Guides, National Cadet Corps, Nehru Yuvak Kendra is noteworthy for effective social mobilization activities in order to create awareness for health and sanitation amongst the rural people; and

(e) to follow instructions for data recording on the structured schedules designed scientifically, on the separate prescribed proforma for reporting information of each household and community/institutional sanitary facilities provided to the beneficiaries as well as the time-frame for reporting by the concerned officials on this programme has also been fixed. This is really a useful exercise for monitoring.

4. UTTAR PRADESH

Allahabad Model

The main thrust of the Government of Uttar Pradesh has been to provide safe drinking water and sanitary facilities at least to one-fourth of rural population by the turn of the century. With a view to attain this goal, the State Sanitation cell was set up in the Department of Panchayati Raj, which initiated its activity of

Rural Sanitation Programme (RSP) in 1984-85 with UNICEF support. Since then, the role of the UNICEF has been related to: (a) dissemination of technical and other information of RSP to the entire State, and (b) to implement low-cost sanitary latrine facilities with organisational support in 13 selected districts only, (out of 63 districts in the State). Out of 13 districts, Allahabad and Sultanpur districts were covered under Intensive Sanitation Project (ISP), with additional hardware and software inputs provided by UNICEF. The Institute of Engineering and Rural Technology (IERT), Allahabad was extended UNICEF support to implement the Rural Sanitation Programme. The operation of Intensive Sanitation Project (ISP) is known as Allahabad Model, as discussed below.

Before discussing the Model, we would briefly discuss the demographic and salient features of the district.

Allahabad district, having a geographical area of 7261 sq. km., comprises a total population of 49.21 lakhs as per 1991 Census (26.24 lakhs males and 22.97 lakhs females). The urban population of 10.22 lakhs is about one-fifth of the total population, whereas majority of people i.e., 38.99 lakhs live in rural areas. The percentage of literacy rate of 42.66 per cent in the district is a little better compared to the State literacy rate of 41.60 per cent but far below the All-India literacy rate of 52.21 per cent Male literacy level of 59.14 per cent in the district is above the State literacy level of 55.73 per cent whereas female literacy rate is below the State literacy rate of 25.31 per cent. On the other hand, urban literacy rate of 69.69 per cent is far above the rural literacy rate of 34.96 per cent.

Major industrial establishments are Indian Farmers Fertilizer Co-operative Ltd., General Electric Co. of India Ltd., Raymond Synthetic Ltd., Geep Industrial Syndicate Ltd., and Tribeni Glass Works Ltd. The district is endowed with silica sands, a major mineral product.

Intensive Sanitation Project (ISP)

With the above background, the Intensive Sanitation Project was initiated, as a pilot project on Rural Sanitation in Sawait Nayana Panchayat, Soraon Block in Allahabad district covering 150 households in 12 revenue villages. The project was implemented, through Gohri Rural Growth Centre, by the Institute of Engineering and Rural Technology (IERT), an NGO of Allahabad, between October 1990 and March 1991. Initially, the main focus of the project was to create awareness amongst the rural community about the need for having sanitary facilities, namely, household latrines, smokeless chulhas, garbage pit, bathing cubicles and soak-pit. It emphasised active participation of the beneficiaries, village level social workers, particularly women, and concerned government officials as well as reduction of the subsidy component as compared to similar programme being implemented in the State of Uttar Pradesh.

For the purpose, the project adopted three different scales of assistance pertaining to sanitation coverage through construction of household latrine. First, subsidy of Rs. 1200 with Rs. 300 from beneficiary as his/her share in construction; second, subsidy of Rs. 450 and the rest from the beneficiary; and third, with only technical guidance and facilities by creating the necessary infrastructure. The IERT and selected Panchayat Udyogs were responsible for adoption of the three different patterns of assistance stated above.

After completing the pilot project in six months, the project activities were extended for a period of three years from 1.8.1992 to 31.7.1995. The project was to cover 12,000 beneficiaries in 250 villages of 8 Community Development Blocks viz., Phulpur, Baheria, Holagarh, Kaudihar, Mauiama, Shankargarh, Soraon and Koraon. It was decided that only those villages will be selected in IERT project, where there is a potential demand for sanitary facilities and they do not fall under the Rural Sanitation Programme of the State government. The main idea was to work out a strategy to reduce the subsidy component while providing the sanitary facilities to the beneficiaries. In fact, the beneficiaries were supposed to get constructed all the five sanitary facilities stated above for which the IERT supplied all the key hardware. After construction of all the sanitary facilities, they were earlier given Rs. 500 as subsidy which has been raised to Rs. 700 after initiation of this project.

Objectives

The main objectives of the project are as follows:

1. To promote awareness about the sanitary practices by motivation and social mobilisation.
2. To provide sanitary facilities by creating demand amongst the beneficiaries.
3. To involve the community in providing sanitation education and training.
4. To promote participation of women in the sanitation programme, and
5. To ensure convergence with other activities of the government programme e.g. water, health, education etc.

Progress Report

The progress report of the IERT, Allahabad project from 1.8.1992 till 20.2.1994 i.e., a period of one year and seven months indicates that:

1. Out of the total target of 12,000 families, 3,060 families were covered (upto 31.12.1993 i.e., within a period of one year four months) where awareness for sanitary education through IEC materials was created;
2. About 1480 persons were trained in the project area such as masons, health workers, project personnel and functionaries of the government/NGOs to promote the programme;
3. Research and Development (R&D) were developed in IERT campus for construction of:

   (i) Low Cost Superstructure for latrines of three alternative materials,
   (ii) Red Clay Glazed W.C. Pan, Foot Rest and Bend for pour-flush latrine,
   (iii) Ferro Cement Precast toilet blocks (including disposal system), and
   (iv) Red Clay half round drainage pipes.

4. Awareness-Generation Programmes were taken up for sanitation drive, special occasion campaign, village school competition, and interaction with schools, group meetings and video shows to promote and motivate the rural people in the project area.

5. Rural Sanitary Marts (RSM) were established at two places viz. one at Gohri village in Soraon Block and another at Koraon Block. These RSM's provide readymade materials for construction of sanitary latrines and other sanitary facilities such as pan and trap, pit cover and pipe etc. Besides, the mart also provides readymade cattle trough, food safe, cheap footwear, soap, nail cutter, cool water pots made of clay of different designs. It also maintains a list of trained masons with their addresses. However, these items of sanitary facilities are manufactured in the RSM and kept for sale on the basis of demand of items either in the project area or even outside.

As discussed earlier in this study, the Intensive Sanitation Programme (ISP) known as Allahabad Model laid the foundation of Rural Sanitation Programme (RSP) in practically all 63 districts of Uttar Pradesh out of which 13 districts were assigned to UNICEF exclusively for implementation of sanitation facilities and services including Allahabad and Sultanpur (as ISP implemented by the Institute of Engineering and Rural Technology – IERT, Allahabad).

The Department of Panchayati Raj of the Government of Uttar Pradesh laid down the basic strategy and guidelines for implementation of Rural Sanitation Programme. As per the Progress Reports (1994-95 onwards till 1996-97) out of yearly allocations made for each district, the strategy was to utilise funds on:

(a) Individual toilets – 7.5%,
(b) Community complexes for women – 10%,
(c) Drainage – 5%, and
(d) Health, education, training and advertisement – 10%.

The Department of Panchayati Raj under Rural Sanitation Programme sanctioned Rs. 2210.31 lakhs during the financial year 1993-94 and the whole amount was released by March 1994. It is stated that during this financial year that a total number of 46,987 individual toilets and 185 community complexes for women were constructed. During 1994-95 an amount of Rs. 4830.67 lakhs was sanctioned and released by the end of March 1995. With this amount, 1,04,488 individual toilets and 585 community complexes for women were constructed. In the financial year 1995-96, a sum of Rs. 6497.35 lakhs was sanctioned for rural sanitation programme, in which Rs. 70.93 lakhs was to be assigned for Ambedkar villages. It was also proposed to construct 2,32,697 individual toilets and 755 community complexes for women and 4,000 community complexes in different schools in the State.

As a part of rural sanitation programme, it has been proposed to construct kharanzas and drainage in rural areas of Uttar Pradesh including Ambedkar villages. The progress made in this direction has still to be assessed.

After Seventh General Election to Panchayats in Uttar Pradesh, a total number of 58,620 Gram Panchayats have been constituted in which Pradhans and members of the panchayat samities have been elected and/or nominated. These 58,620 Gram Panchayats are headed by 19,345 female Pradhans (representing 4,111 SC/ST categories of people, 5,223 Backward classes of people and the rest 10,011 of general caste categories).

Out of the total of 58,620 Gram Panchayats, there are 39,275 male Pradhans (representing 8,347 of SC/ST categories of people, 20,324 of Backward classes of people and the rest 20,324 of general caste categories).

One of the notable achievements of Panchayati Raj in Uttar Pradesh has been that of setting up of Panchayat Udyogs in rural areas to achieve employment avenues for the rural people through different types of cottage and village industries. In fact, this innovative idea was initiated by the UNICEF in many districts of Uttar Pradesh while implementing the Rural Sanitation Programme. The achievement made in different Panchayat Udyogs in Uttar Pradesh from 1994-95 to 1996-97 are given in the Table below:

(Rs. in lakhs)

Year	Target	Production	Sale	Profit
1994-95	2400.00	2509.00	2568.00	129.00
1995-96	2500.00	3041.49	3014.56	162.46
1996-97	2600.00	2501.00	2413.63	139.03

The establishment of Panchayat Udyogs and Sanitary Service Centres or Sanitary Mart from 1991-92 onwards are innovative approaches of the UNICEF in collaboration with the Department of Panchayati Raj. In many districts, the UNICEF has provided revolving fund.

TABLE 2.6
Physical Performance and Usage of Sanitary Facilities

Facility	Intended		Constructed		Existing		In use	
	No.	%	No.	%	No	%	No.	%
Household latrines	50	100	35	70	34	100	26	76
Smokeless Chulhas	50	100	16	32	16	100	7	44
Garbage Pits	50	100	1	2	1	2	1	2
Bathing Cubicles	50	100	6	12	6	100	6	100
Soak-pit	50	100	8	16	8	100	8	100

Source: Evaluation of UNICEF assisted Sanitation Programme in Uttar Pradesh (1984-1991); Operations Research Group, Lucknow, 1993, pp. 65-71.

The Table 2.6 indicates that 35 household latrines were constructed against a target of 50. Out of 35 constructed latrines, 34 latrines exist and 26 latrines (76%) are in use by the beneficiaries. It is seen that other sanitary facilities were not either provided by the project or found to be unacceptable to the beneficiaries as stated in the Evaluation Study.

With regard to training, motivation and social mobilization activities to be followed extensively in the project by different levels of functionaries, the Evaluation Study reveals that out of 50 beneficiaries, 66 per cent stated that the IERT workers persuaded them to get the household latrines and other sanitary facilities installed in their households *(op. cit.*, p. 67). There have been lot of variation in the input materials supplied by IERT to the beneficiaries for constructing latrines for sanitary facilities. About 20 per cent of the beneficiaries stated that they were not provided any material by the IERT (*op. cit.*, p. 68).

With regard to general sanitation, it was reported that waste water was found around 36 per cent in the vicinity of the household, which are soaked by soils invariably. Twenty per cent of the households use tap water and about 74 per cent of the households drink water from wells. 84 per cent of the beneficiaries even now use traditional chulhas and only 14 per cent of the households have adopted smokeless chulhas. Kerosene stove, electric heater and LPG were also being used by some of the beneficiaries.

Conclusion

The two prominent positive features of Allahabad model are:

1. The low cost materials of different designs and specifications for construction of household latrines and sanitary facilities using locally available resources and manufacturing pre-fabricated sanitary materials for the use of beneficiaries as and when demanded may be considered as an example of promoting rural sanitation programme.

2. The training of Master Masons in the IERT campus, who train local masons in different villages as well as some beneficiaries may accelerate the process of construction of latrines and sanitary facilities as and when beneficiaries can afford to purchase pre-fabricated sanitary materials provided by the Sanitary Mart. In this process the element of subsidy can also be reduced considerably or altogether done away with.

Rural Sanitation Programme (RSP) in Uttar Pradesh

As stated earlier, out of 63 districts in Uttar Pradesh, the Rural Sanitation Programme in 13 districts is being assisted by UNICEF and in the rest 50 districts the programme is being implemented by the Department of Panchayati Raj, Government of Uttar Pradesh.

We would briefly discuss about the operations of the UNICEF assisted programme in 13 districts and overall policy of the State Government with regard to promotion of this programme in the State. It also needs to be noted that there had been several changes since the inception of the programme in 1984-85 till 1989-90, particularly in terms of funding pattern of the programme.

1. Since the beginning, the UNICEF financial support to construction of household latrine was restricted upto the plinth level only, as the superstructure including door and roof was supposed to be constructed by the beneficiary. Whereas, the construction of household latrines funded by the State government (with Central government share) the superstructure was constructed. In order to maintain uniformity, the UNICEF funded programme followed the same pattern as that of the State government since 1990.

2. Before 1990, the government programme allocated 50 per cent of the total funds for construction of household latrines for Scheduled Castes/Scheduled Tribes and 30 per cent for the beneficiaries below the poverty line, free of cost. Later, a strategy was evolved during 1990-91 where everyone would pay Rs. 250 as his/her share of contribution in construction of household latrine, the total unit cost of which is estimated as Rs. 2500 in general areas. In difficult problem areas the unit cost was estimated at Rs. 2875 in which the beneficiaries are expected to contribute his/her share as Rs. 287.50 per unit. The Scheduled Castes/Scheduled Tribes beneficiaries are expected to contribute their shares as Rs. 125 in general areas and

Rs. 148 in difficult/problem areas in unit cost of construction of household latrines.

3. Since inception of this programme till 1993-94, it is reported that 40,797 household latrines and 410 women village complexes/latrines (one women village complex costs Rs. 40,700) only have been constructed for which Rs. 8 crores were released by March 31, 1994. There is a proposal to construct another 46,987 household latrines in coming years.

4. The Department of Panchayati Raj has in 63 districts (including Kanpur Rural district) constituted 74,377 Gram Panchayats and 8,805 Nyaya Panchayats in 897 Development Blocks. In these districts, 914 Panchayat Udyogs have been established for implementation of various Rural Development Programmes including Rural Sanitation. These Panchayat Udyogs provide materials for construction of sanitary latrines/facilities and also manufacture wooden furnitures, agricultural implements, cement, tin, etc.

UNICEF Assisted Rural Sanitation Programme

The UNICEF Assisted Rural Sanitation Programme expanded its activities from 1991-92 onwards in 13 districts out of 63 districts. During this period, 43 Panchayat Udyog Rural Sanitation Centres have been established to provide sanitary facilities at household and community levels. UNICEF concentrated its activity of household latrines and sanitary facilities in five out of 13 districts. Till April 1991, in these five districts viz. Allahabad, Sultanpur, Fatehpur, Banda and Lucknow, the achievement was as follows:

District	No. of Household latrines constructed
Allahabad	3,032
Sultanpur	2,744
Fatehpur	2,183
Banda	2,032
Lucknow	2,153
Total	12,144

It is reported that the construction of 12,144 household latrines accounted for over 60 per cent of its activity and it was a major investment made under UNICEF supported programme in the State.

It is in this context, that UNICEF got the Evaluation Study conducted by the Operations Research Group (ORG). As per criteria adopted for sampling and the list of beneficiaries provided, 2,571 beneficiaries (including 50 beneficiary of the IERT Allahabad) in 298 villages of 40 blocks in five districts were selected for interview. Some of the findings with regard to physical performance, installation of household latrines, awareness and acceptance of the programme, general sanitation and community participation convey the effectiveness of implementation strategy and acceptability of the programme as a whole.

The study reveals that the total achievement in construction of household latrines was 49 per cent among the sample beneficiaries. The district-wise performance in latrine construction indicate maximum of 66 per cent in Fatehpur, 60 per cent in Banda, 55 per cent in Lucknow, 35 per cent in Sultanpur and 30 per cent in Allahabad, the lowest. With regard to the materials for household latrines received but not constructed indicated maximum percentage of 48 per cent in Allahabad followed by 10 per cent in Banda, 8 per cent in Sultanpur, 5 per cent in Fatehpur and 1 per cent in Lucknow. Also, the programme was not implemented in 38 per cent of the households in Sultanpur followed by 6 per cent in Allahabad and 3 per cent in Fatehpur (*op. cit.*, p.9).

It is heartening to note that 92 per cent of the beneficiaries were aware about the UNICEF supported programme. The motivation for construction of household latrines and sanitary facilities was done mainly by the Gram Pradhan, along with the panchayat secretary and both played a pivotal role in influencing the people for construction of sanitary latrines/facilities. But the role played by the block level officials, and social workers was insignificant.

The Evaluation Study indicated that the major source of drinking water in the sample villages were found to be wells (44%) handpump of different types (29%), handpump of India Mark-II (15%) and piped water supply (11%). Pucca drains (7%) and Kutcha drains into pond (29%) existed. The garbage around the houses (28%) are general features of sanitation in the sample villages.

Conclusion

It is indeed heartening to note that 92 per cent of the beneficiaries were aware about UNICEF supported programme. In regard to creating awareness and motivation amongst the people, the role played by the Gram Pradhan and the Panchayat Secretary were crucial. However, the role played by Block Development Officials, social workers and others was found to be insignificant. Inspite of all these efforts, the Evaluation Study observed that the "Community participation in the entire process has been limited. Perhaps, the root cause for the same lies in the process of selection of beneficiaries in which only those were selected who showed willingness to pay for the latrines. It was not implemented as a community decision in the village and for every beneficiary it remained as individual cost benefit analysis,. At a later stage of the programme, lack of concerted and committed efforts in providing IEC about the programme (which included general sanitation) also did not help the cause of community participation" (*op. cit.*, p.19).

B. WORLD BANK ASSISTED PROGRAMMES

5. GUJARAT

Rural Sanitation Programme

Gujarat is one of the pioneering States to implement low cost sanitation scheme. The conversion of dry-latrines into pour-flush latrines was initiated by the Government of Gujarat in collaboration with Harijan Sewak Sangh and its sister organisation Safai Vidyalaya (Environmental Sanitation Institute). It is claimed that Gujarat achieved 99 per cent conversion of dry-latrines in urban areas under Bhangi Kastha Mukti Programme. However, it is said that adequate provision of sanitary latrines and safe drinking water is a monumental task even now, in urban and rural areas of Gujarat, due to growth of population and consequent increase in number of houses, needing basic facilities like low cost sanitation and safe-drinking water for a healthy living.

When low cost sanitation scheme was launched in 1961, the total population of the State was 2.06 crores, out of which 53 lakh people were living in 181 urban towns/cities and 153 lakh people in 18,584 villages. The total population of the State was recorded as 3.41 crores in 1981 Census and 4.14 crores in 1991 Census i.e. a decadal increase of 22.82 per cent. Presently, the State covers an area of 187,091 sq. km constituting 19 districts and 216 urban towns/cities in which about 84 lakh people are living. There are 18,275 villages in the State in which about 330 lakh people live. It is estimated that there are about 14.17 lakh houses in urban areas and 54.50 lakh in rural areas, assuming an average of 6 persons per house, both in urban and rural areas. It is further estimated that 40 per cent i.e. about 5.67 lakh houses in urban areas are having latrine facility while 8.50 lakh houses need conversion/construction of sanitary latrines. In rural areas 3 per cent i.e. 1.64 lakh houses only have latrine facility and about 52.86 lakh need sanitary latrines.

Experimental Low Cost Sanitation Programmes

Keeping in view, the magnitude of environmental degradation and sanitation problems in urban and rural areas caused by disposal of liquid and solid waste in habitated areas, water shortage and financial stringency of the local bodies, the Government of Gujarat launched the low cost sanitation programmes as a workable solution to these problems with the financial and organisational support of the World Bank, UNICEF and Government of Netherlands. It is significant to note that the Government of Gujarat took minimal support from the Government of India and that too only recently. These programmes are discussed briefly below:

(a) *World Bank Assistance for Urban Low Cost Sanitation Programme (Under IDA-CR - 1280 IN)*

The World Bank assistance was provided to Gujarat Water Supply and Sewerage Board (GWSSB) for implementation of programme in collaboration with the local bodies and user households under the guidance of Ishwarbhai Patel a dedicated Gandhian social worker and Hony. Advisor to this programme and Director of Safai Vidyalaya, Ahmedabad.

Implementation and Financial Assistance Pattern: The implementation of the programme began after procedures, organisational strategy, coordination of different agencies, and a norm of financial assistance pattern were adopted by the GWSSB. The main component of the Financial Assistance Pattern for a unit of sanitary latrine in 58 selected project towns towards grants-in-aid to the beneficiaries was worked out as follows:

(In Rupees)

(a)	Total cost of Urban P.F. Latrine included	
	Net estimated cost	2291.00
	+ E.T.P. Charges	409.00
		2700.00
	Note: E.T.P. Charges of Rs. 409 were disbursed by GWSSB as follows.	409.00
	Promotional aid for popularising the programme per latrine to Beneficiaries	125.00
	Local Bodies	125.00
	GWSSB (Retains for operating the programme)	159.00
		409.00
(b)	Grant-in-aid per latrine was worked out as follows:	
(i)	Beneficiary categories of SC/ST/EBC @ 75 per cent of	
	Net estimated cost of Rs. 2291.00 for capital	1718.25
	Incentive grant towards E.T.P.	125.00
		1843.25
	Say	1850.00
	Beneficiaries own resources investment/latrine worked out to (Rs. 2291-1718=573)	573.00
(ii)	Beneficiaries of other categories For others @ 50 per cent of	
	Net estimated cost of Rs. 2291 for capital	1145.50
	Incentive grant towards E.T.P	125.00
	Beneficiaries own resource investment latrine worked out to	1270.50
	(Rs. 2291.00 - 1145.50 = 1145.50)	1145.50

Source : GWSSB, Gandhinagar, (Gujarat).

Progress in Implementation: It is reported that the programme was divided into two stages with a total target of 30,000 pour-flush latrines to be constructed/converted. In the first stage, it was planned to construct 26,780 P.F. latrines including conversion of 6,269 units of dry-latrines as well as 440 community dry-latrines. The remaining units of the total target was to be taken up in the second stage. In all, 58 towns were selected. Initially, 15 towns were selected with a target of 11,875 units of latrines to be constructed/converted and later on 43 towns were added with a target of 18,125 units. It is reported that from inception of the project till January 1992, in 15 towns, 10,959 units of latrines were constructed (i.e 90.3 per cent of the target) and 430 units were under progress. During the same period the progress achieved in 43 towns is stated as construction of 16,169 units of pour-flush latrines (i.e 89.20 per cent of the target) and 1,650 units of latrines were under various stages of construction. In other words in both the stages, 27,128 latrines were constructed (90.43%) and 2,872 latrines were yet to be constructed out of the total target of 30,000 units. It is further reported that by March 1992, 29,949 latrines were constructed out of the target of 30,000 latrines in these projects towns, thus almost meeting the target.

(b) *World Bank Assistance for Rural Low Cost Sanitation Programme (Under IDA-CR-1643-IN)*

This programme was also assisted by the World Bank, and implemented through the GWSSB and with the joint-efforts of selected local NGOs/ voluntary Agencies selected and trained by the Environmental Sanitation Institute (ESI), in which it played an important role as Nodal Agency under the guidance of Director of Safai Vidyalaya, Ahmedabad. The programme was initiated in April 1989 for a period of about 5 years, and continued upto July 1994.

Implementation and Financial Assistance Pattern: The role of each participatory agency along with strategies, steps and procedures were defined for implementation of the programme. The involvement of selected local Voluntary Agencies for construction of sanitary latrines in rural households was considered as a desirable factor in view of their direct contact with the people, who could be easily motivated by them to have this facility. The GWSSB framed a policy for giving grant-in-aid for which financial assistance pattern was devised as follows:

		In Rupees	
A.	Total Cost of Rural P.F. latrine included		
	Net estimated cost	2291.00	
	+ E.T.P. Charges	409.00	
		2700.00	2700.00

Note: E.T.P Charges were disbursed by the GWSSB as follows:

	Promotional aid for popularising the programme per latrine	
	Beneficiaries	125.00
	Nodal Agency (ESI)	100.00
	Implementing Local NGOs	100.00
	GWSSB (Retains) for operating the programme	84.00
		409.00
B.	Grants-in-aid per latrine was worked out as follows:	
(i)	Beneficiary categories of SC/ST/EBC @ 75 per cent of Net estimated cost of Rs. 2291 for capital	1718.25
	Incentive grant toward E.T.P.	125.00
		1843.25
	Say	1850.00
	Beneficiaries own resource investment/latrine worked out to (Rs. 2291.00-1718.00=573.00)	573.00
(ii)	Beneficiaries of other categories @ 50 per cent of	
	–Net estimated cost of Rs. 2291 for capital	1145.00
	–Incentive grant towards E.T.P	125.00
	–Beneficiaries own resource investment worked out to (Rs. 2291.00 - 1145.50)	1145.00

(*Source:* GWSSB, Gandhinagar, Gujarat)

Financial Support for Implementation of the Programme (April 1989 to July 1994): The Table 2.7 indicates that from April 1989, to July 1994 the Gujarat Water Supply and Sewerage Board (GWSSB) provided grants to the Environmental Sanitation Institute (ESI), the Nodal Agency, to the tune of Rs. 11.81 crores, for implementation of the programme by different Voluntary Organisations. The expenditure incurred during this period has been of the order of Rs. 12.01 crores. In other words, the ESI had to receive additional grant of about Rs. 20.80 lakhs. Further, the Table indicates that during this period a total number of 67,233 latrines were constructed (out of a total target of 70,000 units), for which subsidy was paid to the concerned beneficiaries. It also shows that from April 1993 to July 1994 the GWSSB provided grants to the ESI to the tune of Rs. 3.32 crores, out of which the total expenditure incurred was over Rs. 2.46 crores for the construction of 14,136 latrines under the Minimum Needs Programme (MNP) and the total expenditure of about Rs. 1.15 crores incurred for the construction of 5,220 latrines under the Central Rural Sanitation Programme (CRSP). It is interesting to note that the GWSSB promoted the programme of the MNP and the CRSP of the Department of Rural Development, Government of India under the World Bank (IDA-1643 IN) assisted programme. Presumably, this process may have accelerated the pace of construction of rural sanitary latrines in Gujarat.

Further Progress Achieved: It is reported that the programme was well accepted by the rural people from its very inception in April 1989. In all, 127 local NGOs/Voluntary Agencies were involved in 19 districts of Gujarat for covering 2,382 villages of 145 blocks for construction of 68,596 pour-flush latrines in rural households under the guidance/supervision of the Environmental Sanitation Institute and the GWSSB. Out of the total target of 70,000 rural pour-flush latrines, it is reported that during the programme period, 68,596 units had already been constructed and 900 units were in various stages of construction. For the rest 504 units sanitary sets/grants have been supplied. It is to be noted further that out of 68,596 units of rural pour-flush latrines, 39,991 units were constructed for SC/ST/EBC categories, 22,687 for other categories and the rest 5,918 units

TABLE 2.7

Statement showing financial and physical details of IDA - 1643 IN in Rural Sanitation Project in Gujarat from January 1989 to July 1994

(In Rupees)

Sl. No.	Years	Grants Received from GWSS Board	Total Expenditure	Total No. of Latrines constructed
1.	January 1989 to March 1990	2,00,00,000	1,89,20,500	11,035
2.	April 1990 to March 1991	2,00,00,000	2,00,26,300	12,261
3.	April 1991 to March 1992	2,30,00,000	2,33,15,950	12,706
4.	April 1992 to March 1993	2,19,37,250	2,17,29,650	11,865
5.	April 1993 to March 1994	2,17,07,600		
	(a) MNP		1,85,07,820	10,380
	(b) CRSP *		39,42,400	1,792
6.	April 1994 to July 1994	1,15,00,000		
	(a) MNP		61,45,280	3,756
	(b) SP		75,41,600	3,428
	Total	11,81,44,850	12,01,29,500	67,223

Note: MNP (Minimum Needs Programme) of Government of India started from April 1993 and continued upto July 1994

* CRSP(Central Rural Sanitation Programme) of Government of India started from January 1994 and continued upto July 1994.

Source: Report of the World Bank Cell, GWSSB, Gandhinagar & Environmental Sanitation Institute, Ahmedabad on Sanitary Latrines for Rural Areas in Gujarat State (Under IDA Credit No. 1643 IN) April 1989 to July 1994, pp. 25 to 30.

under the Minimum Needs Programme (MNP) and Central Rural Sanitation Programme (CRSP) during this period, (as stated in the Report of Environmental Sanitation Institute,

Ahmedabad and the World Bank cell of the Gujarat Water Supply and Sewerage Board, Gandhinagar).

Environmental Sanitation Institute, ESI (or Safai Vidyalaya), Gandhi Ashram, Ahmedabad is the only notable NGO in Gujarat, which has been involved in Environmental Sanitation and Health Programmes in rural and urban areas since 1963. Many projects in Gujarat, sponsored and funded by international organizations (viz. World Bank, UNICEF, WHO, Indo-Dutch etc.) were implemented by the ESI for improving environmental sanitation and health status of the people. In the implementation process, the ESI took help and cooperation of local NGOs and grassroot institutions for people's participation. One of the main objectives of the ESI is to create awareness in the minds of the people about Low Cost Sanitation programmes in general and for women and children in particular.

Recently, the National Dairy Development Board (NDDB), UNICEF and ESI under joint collaboration took up the health and sanitation programmes to train motivators and Master Masons. Nearly 100 motivators and 40 Master Masons have been trained in Baroda and Surat districts. This programme also included the Rural Sanitary Marts (RSMs) at selected centres of these districts. It is reported that the programme has proved to be very useful for women and children and hopefully this may be taken up in other districts also.

The main activity profile as reported by the Environmental Sanitation Institute, Ahmedabad to promote low cost sanitation and health programmes as an implementation strategy to promote environmental sanitation in Gujarat from 1963 to 1997 is summarised in Table 2.8.

One of the main activities of the ESI from 1988 onwards has been that of implementation of construction of low cost latrines with funds provided by the World Bank through the Gujarat Water Supply and Sewerage Board (GWSSB) and with funds from other international organisations. (Such as UNICEF, WHO) or funds from central and State governments from 1988-89 onwards. The aggregate amount of financial assistance received and the total expenditure incurred from 1988-89 to 1996-97 for construction of 1,24,841 low cost latrines has been shown in Table 2.9.

TABLE 2.8
Activity Profile of Environmental Sanitation Institute
(1963 to 1997)

Sl. No.	Item of Activity	Achievement (Nos.)
1.	Training Camps	1997
2.	Training Programmes for Engineers	97
3.	Persons trained	85684
4.	Water seal latrines (Bawala type) constructed	17500
5.	Soakpits constructed	65500
6.	Bathing platforms constructed	41000
7.	Ventilators provided	50000
8.	Conversion of dry latrines to water seal latrines	186000
9.	Smokeless stoves (chulhas) constructed	52250
10.	Model ground prepared (financed by Unicef)	23
11.	Toilet connected with biogas plants	15270
12.	Latrines constructed in villages through 145 NGOs upto March 1997	124841
13.	Latrines constructed in 55 towns under GWSSB, IDA-1280-IN	29949
14.	Latrines constructed under Urban Sanitation Project in 97 towns	22943
15.	Latrines constructed in urban areas under AMC IDA-1643 -IN	1428
16.	Sanitation Packages executed under ICDS Projects at Anganwadi centres in villages	478
17.	Indo-Dutch Pilot in two villages (Sanitation Packages provided)	142
18.	Water Awareness Project under World Bank (Villages)	50
19.	Baseline survey for Water & Sanitation (districts)	4

Source: Environmental Sanitation Institute, Gandhi Ashram, Ahmedabad.

TABLE 2.9

Abstract of Advance Given by Gujarat Water Supply and Sewerage Board under MNP and CRSP Programmes

Sl. No.	Financial Year	Opening Balance of Advance Rs.	Total Amount of Advance Rs.	Total Amount Rs.	Total Latrines Rs.	Total Expenditure Rs.	Balance of Advance Rs.	Remarks
1	2	3	4	5	6	7	8	9
1	1988-89	-	1500000	1500000	-	-	(+) 15,00,000	MNP
2	1989-90	1500000	18500000	2000000	11035	18920500	(+) 10,79,500	MNP
3	1990-91	1079500	2200000	23079500	12261	20026300	(+) 30,53,200	MNP
4	1991-92	3053200	23000000	26053200	12706	23315950	(+) 23,37,250	MNP
5	1992-93	2737250	19200000	21937250	11865	21729650	(+) 2,07,600	
6	1993-94	207600	21500000	21707600	10380 MNP	18507820		
					1792 CRSP	3941900	(-) 7,42,120	MNP + CRSP
					12172	22449720		
7	1994-95	-742120	27000000	26257880	6145 MNP	10062320		
					6922 CRSP	15228400	(+) 9,67,160	MNP + CRSP
8	1995-96	964960	53000000	53964960	8114 MNP	13076360		
					18621 CRSP	40966200		
					-----------	-----------		
					26735	54042560	(-) 77,600	MNP + CRSP

Contd.

TABLE 2.9 *(Contd.)*

1	2	3	4	5	6	7	8	9
9	1996-97	-77600	49000000	48922400	7351 MNP	11575610		
					17649 CRSP	38827800		
					25,000	50403410	(-) 14,81,010	MNP + CRSP
					124841	236178810		
					79857 MNP	137214510		
					44984 CRSP	98964300		
			234700000		124841	236178810		

MNP: Minimum Needs Programme. CRSP: Central Rural Sanitation Programme.
Source: Environmental Sanitation Institute, Gandhi Ashram, Ahmedabad.

(c) *UNICEF Assistance Programme for Control of Diarrhoeal Diseases, Water Supply and Sanitation (CDD-WATSAN)*

The programme is operating in Panchmahal district of Gujarat State with UNICEF assistance. Panchmahal district is located in the middle of eastern part of Gujarat. It is a drought-prone district. The headquarters of the district is Godhra town, a distance of 169 km from the State capital. There are 9 towns, 11 talukas and 1,895 villages in the district.

The total population of the district is 29.49 lakhs according to 1991 Census. Out of this, the urban population constitute 11.89 per cent only, which is lowest in the State. Scheduled Tribes constitute 41.76 per cent of the total district population, compared with overall State population of 20 per cent. The literacy rate is 36.17 per cent only in which female literacy rate is 22.60 per cent Due to poor quality of land, shortage of rainfall, lack of income generation activities, there is high rate of seasonal out-migration to find alternate source of income.

It is estimated that over 12 lakh cases of diarrhoea occur every year in the district, in which a child below five years suffers from diarrhoea 3 times on an average every year. Diarrhoea causes loss of appetite leading to malnutrition and further infection, particularly amongst children. It is reported that 2.06 to 4.93 per cent are affected with malnutrition (due to protein deficiency) which is related to diarrhoeal diseases caused by lack of safe-drinking water and sanitation facilities in different talukas of the district.

It is in the above context the CDD-WATSAN approach laid down strategies to achieve the objectives of the programme in Panchmahal district.

Strategies: The main strategies adopted were: (a) to utilise existing organizational and infrastructure of the district such as water, sanitation, health, ICDS, education, nutrition etc. of the government along with the UNICEF financial support initiative of CDD-WATSAN for planning and implementation purposes; (b) to involve NGOs in such areas for creation of awareness, motivation; and (c) to ensure participation of beneficiaries in planning, implementation, maintenance and evaluation, particularly women.

Objectives and Interventions: In order to attain the main objectives of CDD-WATSAN programme, some guidelines for intervention have been laid down:

(a) to make available at least one handpump within 0.5 km distance for safe drinking water supply to household and institutional levels by ensuring its maintenance and supervision by trained mechanic/sanitation motivator, preferably a woman at each village panchayat level;
(b) to create awareness for the use of clean water, sanitation, excreta and solid waste disposal at the household and institutional levels;
(c) to establish Sanitary Mart in each taluka with atleast 8 to 12 masons including Master Mason for providing sanitary facilities; and
(d) to establish ORS depot in each village and ORT corners in each PHC and CHC with trained health workers as well as Diarrhoea Treatment Training Unit (DTTV) at district hospital not only for the CDD purposes but also for immunization, measles vaccination and overall health care, particularly of children below 5 years and the rural community as a whole.

The CDD-WATSAN project also suggests various methods of prevention and management of diarrhoeal diseases by the use of safe-drinking water, and safe-disposal of excreta, particularly of children and solid waste through IEC activities as well as formation and proper functioning of CDD-WATSAN committees at the village level.

(d) *Indo-Dutch Pilot Project*

The Indo-Dutch Pilot Project was undertaken in collaboration with the Government of India, Government of Gujarat and the Government of the Netherlands as a Rural Sanitation Programme. After discussion with the authorities of the Gujarat Water Supply and Sewerage Board, it was decided to cover three districts, viz., Amreli, Banaskantha and Mehsana under the project.

The project is in two phases covering seven talukas viz., Lathi and Libiya talukas of Amreli district, Kankrej, Radhanpur and Santalpur talukas in Banaskantha district, and Hari and Sami talukas in Mehsana district in phase one. These 7 talukas of 3 districts covers 163 villages with a total population of 2,59,141 having 45,908 households. It is proposed to provide 7500 household latrines with bath and soak-pits to those beneficiaries expressing felt need. Phase two, constitutes the same 7 talukas of the same districts (as in phase one). Phase two covers 104 villages with a total population of 71,215 and 11,869 households. In phase two, it is proposed to create health awareness and demand for sanitary facilities, i.e., latrines (including bath and soak-pits) to the limit of 20,000 units in all including 7500 units provided in phase one. It is also proposed that as soon as 7500 latrines are constructed under phase one, the phase two programme will begin operating.

Conclusion

Gujarat is one of the leading States in tackling rural sanitation programme with involvement of NGOs and local level voluntary organisations. Yet the exploding population poses further challenges to resolve the problems of sanitation and health in rural areas. This calls for involvement of Panchayati Raj institutions besides NGOs and voluntary organisations.

6. KARNATAKA

Rural Water Supply and Sanitation Programme

The Rural Water Supply and Environmental Sanitation Project in Karnataka was initiated in the year 1994, in collaboration with the Government of India, State Government and the World Bank for a period of seven years (1994 to 2000) as a part of central assistance to States for development projects. The funds provided by the World Bank has the standard terms for repayment of loan in 35 years maturity, with a grace of 10 years.

Objectives

The main objectives of the project are:

(a) to expand accessibility of potable Water Supply System and ensure environmental sanitation facilities for improving health status of rural people in order to increase their productivity and quality of life; and
(b) to ensure beneficiary participation in operation and maintenance, including cost recovery responsibility by the people and concerned agencies implementing the project.

Components

The main components of the project are:

(a) to rehabilitate existing Water Supply System, which need leakage repair and to construct new water supply borewell programmes by introducing water quality monitoring and ground water recharge measures for the Public Health Engineering Department of the State;
(b) to construct sanitation facilities viz., sullage drains, pour-flush latrines, washing platforms, cattle troughs, bathing cubicles, street bins and bio-gas plants as per demand of individual household and community as a whole;
(c) to create awareness amongst the people for improved domestic and community hygiene by constituting village water supply and sanitation committees as well as to train the motivators and functionaries associated with the implementation of the project; and
(d) to involve Non-Governmental Organizations (NGOs) in planning and implementation of environmental sanitation and health communication areas of the project.

Implementation Strategy

It is expected that the project would provide safe-drinking water supply and improved sanitation along with health education to about 4 crore and 80 lakh people in 1200 villages of 16 project districts. It might have considerable impact on the quality of life of the rural people in terms of health status and environmental sanitation, which would accelerate their economic pursuits and productivity.

In order to achieve the objectives, the project has laid down some principles for implementation strategies, such as:

(a) to ensure market mechanism for sale of low cost sanitary models to the beneficiaries on demand in the project villages, suitable to their requirement; and
(b) to train local masons for ensuring quality control in latrine construction.

It has been assumed that about 90,000 units of Two-Pit Pour-Flush latrine (TPPF) might be installed in the project villages. The total project cost of Rs. 36.28 crores has been estimated (including the base cost of Rs. 32.31 crores) for construction of TPPF latrines with superstructure by using bricks for walls and G.I. sheets for door and roofs as well as schemes for rural water supply, health, communication etc. (Refer Table 2.10). It is significant to mention that the State government has introduced an element of subsidy in the total cost of Rs. 2400 of one unit of household latrine. The extent of subsidy is: (a) Rs. 1650 for SC/ST/EWS categories; and (b) Rs. 1200 for all other categories. It is reported that 50 per cent of the subsidy would be paid after the latrine is constructed upto to the plinth level and the remaining 50% after completion of the superstructure. One of the special features of the programme has been to create awareness amongst the beneficiaries to use the latrine for which they have to contribute their labour or own resources towards construction. Nevertheless, the full amount of subsidy is given to each beneficiary which is being monitored by the Project Cells of the Zilla Parishad Engineering Wings (ZPEW) having complete responsibility for implementation of the project in terms of policy guidelines, technical assistance, training, utilization of funds, contribution to beneficiaries etc.

Financial Planning

The financial planning for the utilization of funds to be provided by State government, World Bank and IDA assistance as well as contribution from beneficiaries have been estimated for different sectors in order to compute the total project cost for seven years i.e., from 1994 to 2000 as shown in Tables 2.10, 2.11 and 2.12.

TABLE 2.10
Estimated Cost

(in Million Rupees)

Sl. No.	Items	Local	Foreign	Total	Percentage to total Project Cost
1.	Rural Water Supply	1647.80	289.52	1937.32	53.40
2.	Environmental Sanitation	760.76	43.12	803.88	22.16
3.	Health Communication & Institutional Strengthening	150.92	15.40	166.32	4.58
4.	Project Support Studies	289.52	33.88	323.40	8.91
5.	Total Base Cost	2849.00	381.92	3230.92	89.05
6.	Physical & Price Contingencies	317.24	80.08	397.32	10.95
7	TOTAL PROJECT COST	3166.24	462.00	3628.24	100.00

Note: One US Dollar has been converted as Rs. 30.80

TABLE 2.11
Financial Plan

(in Million Rupees)

Sl. No.	Source	Local	Foreign	Total	Percentage to total Project Cost
1.	Government	517.44	–	517.44	14.26
2.	Community	277.20	–	277.20	7.64
3.	IDA	2371.60	462.00	2833.60	78.10
4	Total	3166.24	462.00	3628.24	100.00

Note: (i) One US Dollar has been converted as Rs. 30.80
(ii) The above costs include an estimated Rs.338.80 million in taxes and duties.

TABLE 2.12
Estimate Disbursement

(Annual in Million Rupees)

Sl. No.	IDA Financial Year	1992	1993	1994	1995	1996	1997	1998
1	2	3	4	5	6	7	8	9
1.	Annual	252.56	489.80	631.40	656.04	572.88	187.88	40.04
2.	Cumulative	252.56	745.36	1376.76	2032.80	2605.18	2793.56	2833.60

Note: (i) Economic Rate of Return (ERR) not applicable
(ii) One US Dollar has been converted as Rs. 30.80.

The total project cost has been estimated as Rs. 36.28 crores out of which the financial contribution from local sources accounts for Rs. 31.66 crores (87.27%) and foreign sources Rs. 4.62 crores (12.73%) only. The local sources constitute financial contribution from government 14.26 per cent, communities 7.64 per cent and International Development Agencies (IDA) 65.37 per cent, and foreign sources 12.73 per cent. In other words, in the total project costs, the Government and communities financial contribution accounts for about 22 per cent and that of IDA and foreign sources 78 per cent. Further, out of the total project cost of Rs. 36.28 crores, the total base cost of Rs. 32.31 crores (89.09%) excluding the allocation to physical and price contingencies as Rs. 3.97 crores (10.95%) have been assessed for different components of the project. In order of priorities, four components of the project have been allocated funds in the total project cost such as Rural Water Supply (53.40%), Environmental Sanitation (22.16), Project Support Studies (8.91%) and Health, Communication and Institutional Strengthening (4.58%) only. (See Tables 2.10 and 2.11)

The estimated amount of about Rs. 28.33 crores (78.10%) in this project to be obtained from foreign and IDA sources have been assessed for disbursement annually from 1994 to 2000 (See Table 2.12).

The Integrated Rural Water Supply and Environmental Sanitation Project taken up in 1994 in 1202 villages in the jurisdiction of 16 districts of Bangalore (R), Tumkur, Shimoga, Mysore, Mandya, Hassan, Dakshina Kannada, Belgaum, Bidar, Gulbarga, Raichur, Bellary, Davanagore, Koppal, Chamarajanagar and Udupi has achieved reasonable progress.

Implementation in Pilot Phase started in 1993 and water supply works in 10 pilot schemes have been completed and the community is maintaining the schemes after collecting necessary tariff for Operation and Maintenance. Environmental Sanitation work was completed in 8 villages and are under progress in the remaining three villages. By May 1998, the following 71 water supply schemes were commissioned.

Further, work in 64 villages have been completed and are ready for commissioning as detailed below.

All the water supply work under Phase-I are expected to be completed by the end of December 1998.

Environmental Sanitation

This component includes surface drains for sullage, bathing cubicles, cattle troughs, washing platforms, individual latrines, street dustbins. The Village Water Supply and Sanitation Committee constituted in each project village will decide the mode of execution of Environmental Sanitation Work in their respective villages. The district-wise details of Environmental Sanitation work under progress and the individual sanitary latrines constructed are:

Phase II

Under Phase II of the project, the details of tenders awarded are given below.

Community Contribution

For Phase I villages the communities were to mobilize a sum of Rs. 466.40 lakhs as their share in the form of cash/material/labour towards environmental sanitation work. By May 1998 a sum of Rs. 321.71 lakhs in cash as against an agreed cash contribution of Rs. 386.55 lakh was mobilised. The balance is proposed to be mobilized in the form of material and labour from the communities.

The communities have mobilised a sum of Rs. 482.95 lakhs in Phase II villages so far.

Ground Water Recharge Measures

By May 1998, treatment for 100 micro watersheds were completed and another 34 new micro watersheds had been taken up for treatment. It was envisaged to take up another 71 micro watersheds for treatment during the current year. An amount of Rs. 626 lakhs has already been spent under this component.

Training

Training is a very important component under the project. It basically concentrates on the development of human resources and involving the community in efficient implementation and operation and maintenance of the facilities created in the project villages for long-term sustainability and improved quality of life. The one year training programme was completed at a cost of Rs. 75.36 lakhs and 5,419 persons were trained/oriented in 10 project districts. A total number of 8,200 Government Servants, teachers and other persons in the project villages are proposed for training during these two years. During the period from December 1996 to April 1998 in all 955 training programmes were conducted and 5,290 persons in the categories of Primary School Teachers, Caretakers, Masons, Pipelayer/Valvemen, Engineers, Accounts Personnel and Senior Administrative Personnel have been trained. In addition, 7,068 persons including Primary School Teachers and Hand Pump Care Takers have also attended the orientation session.

Community Participation

Community Participation at all stages is one of the main objectives of the Project. For ensuring involvement of communities in planning, implementation and O & M of the completed schemes, the Staff Appraisal Report of the project provide for involvement of NGOs for conducting PRAs, Community Participation activities, constitution of VWSCs and assisting the VWSCs in mobilisation of contribution towards environmental sanitation activities. NGOs have been involved in the project from 1993. With effect from December 1997 fresh contracts have been entered into with the NGOs for the Project Districts.

Health Sanitation and Hygiene Education

This component aims at creation of greater community awareness about water related health problems and to create individual and community demand for safe water, improved hygiene and environmental sanitation activities. The Department of Health and Family Welfare is implementing this component in Shimoga district. In the remaining project districts, the HSHE activities are being implemented through district NGOs with a State level apex consultant. The services of M/s. STEM, Bangalore has been procured as a consultant for implementation of this component in the remaining 11 project districts.

During July and August 1997 two workshops were conducted by District Health Officer, Shimoga and prepared IEC prototype printed materials. Health Department in Shimoga is making necessary arrangements for mass production of IEC materials. Five-day foundation and orientation workshop was organised for preparation of district and village level action plan from 27-31 January, 1998 at Bangalore and a regional workshop for production of prototype printed IEC materials was organised in Gulbarga.

Conclusion

This long-term externally aided Water Supply and Environmental Sanitation Project holds prospects of meeting one of the basic needs of the masses in a substantial manner. In the absence of feedback, we are unable to make any definite assessment. The Panchayati Raj Institutions are involved in the implementation of various components of the projects.

7. MAHARASHTRA

Rural Water Supply and Sanitation Programme

The Rural Water Supply and Environmental Sanitation Project was initiated in the year 1992 in collaboration with the Government of India, Government of Maharashtra and the World Bank for a period of seven years (1992 to 2000) as a part of Central assistance to States for development projects. The funds provided by the World Bank have the standard terms of repayment of loan in 35 years maturity.

Objectives

The main objectives of the project are as follows:

(a) to expand accessibility of potable water supply systems and environmental sanitation facilities for improving health status of rural people in order to increase their productivity and quality of life; and

(b) to strrngthen operational and maintenance structure by establishing Government and NGO Task Force to ensure beneficiary participation and cost recovery responsibility by the people and concerned agencies implementing the project.

Implementation Strategy Components

The project has been undertaken in 10 districts in Maharashtra with implementation strategies laid down as:

(a) to ensure market mechanism for sale of materials of two-pit pour-flush latrine model on demand basis along with accessories for piped water supply to the beneficiaries in the project villages of 10 selected districts, and

(b) to train sufficient number of masons for construction of Pour Flush latrines based on standard quality and specifications.

In the 10 project districts, 1,042 villages have been identified in order of priorities for installation of P.F. latrines along with piped water supply. Among the priorities, (a) 316 project villages, (having population of 1500 or above) have been selected, which comprises a population of about 14 lakhs (b) 126 project villages (having population between 1000-1500) have been identified for covering total population of about 2 lakhs only, and (c) Non-project 600 villages have also been selected (having population of 1000 or above), constituting a total population of about 19 lakhs, in which P.F. latrines is being constructed at owners cost with a subsidy provided by government. In other words, the World Bank involvement is only in 442 project villages with regard to both facilities i.e., installation of P.F. latrines and provision of piped water supply. But the World Bank is involved in all the 1,042 identified villages in 10 districts of the State for provision of piped water supply.

In regard to safe drinking water, the project emphasises firstly to expand access to potable water supply system in the project districts by providing: (a) 75 large regional piped water supply schemes; (b) 170 individual village piped water supply schemes; and (c) installation of about 3,000 India Mark-III handpumps. Secondly, in order to promote environmental sanitation and health communication components the project has evolved some implementation strategies for disposal of waste water in villages and improved drainage and installation of low cost latrines by creating awareness in village community for individual and community hygiene through the joint-efforts of the NGO and the Department of Public Health.

The average cost of P.F. latrines is estimated at Rs. 2,100 only (at 1990 prices). While constructing the latrine, subsidy is provided: (a) for Scheduled Castes and Tribes by the Government of Maharashtra @ Rs. 1080 and by Zilla Parishad @ Rs 360. The rest of the amount of Rs 660 has to be met by the beneficiaries; (b) for all other categories of people, subsidy @ Rs. 1,080 only is provided by the Government of Maharashtra, the rest amount of Rs 1020 has to be met by the beneficiaries. As a principle, 50 per cent of the subsidy is being given after the latrine is constructed upto plinth level and the remaining 50 per cent after completion of the superstructure. Full subsidy is given to each beneficiary irrespective of type of P.F. latrines construction or their contribution in the form of labour or material.

The primary responsibility for implementing the project is that of the Zilla Parishad of each district, which assign the supervisory responsibility of implementation and monitoring jointly to the Junior Engineer (Works) and Block Development Officer. Selected NGOs are assigned responsibility to create awareness about the programme and promote both the schemes of latrine installation and piped water supply schemes amongst the individual household and village communities.

Financial Planning

The financial planning for the utilization of funds to be provided by the Government of Maharashtra, District Council, World Bank, IDA and Household contribution have been estimated for different sectors in order to arrive at the total project cost for seven years i.e from 1992 to 1998 as shown in Tables 2.13, 2.14 and 2.15 below:

TABLE 2.13
Estimated Costs

(Million Rupees)

Sl. No.	Items	Local	Foreign	Total	Percentage to total Project Cost
1.	Rural Water Supply Schemes	2214.52	437.36	2651.88	61.19
2.	Sanitation Programme	274.12	12.32	286.44	6.61
3.	Project Support	49.28	3.08	52.36	1.21
4.	Institution Building	123.20	43.12	166.32	3.84
5.	Health Communication	144.76	15.40	160.16	3.69
6.	Other Consultant Services	18.48	3.08	21.56	0.50
7.	International Staff Salaries (ZP/GSDA/DOPH)	117.04	21.56	138.60	3.20
8.	MWSSB Engineering Costs	363.44	64.68	428.12	9.88
9.	Land Acquisition	6.16		6.16	0.14
10.	Total Base Costs	3311.00	600.60	3911.60	90.26
11.	Physical contingencies	234.08	43.12	277.20	6.40
12.	Price contingencies	52.36	92.40	144.76	3.34
13.	Total Project Costs	3597.44	736.12	4333.56	100.00

Note: (i) One US Dollar has been converted as Rs. 30.80 ps.
(ii) The above costs include an estimated Rs. 397.32 million taxes and duties

TABLE 2.14
Financial Plan

(in Million Rupees)

Sl. No.	Sources	Local	Foreign	Total	Percentage to total Project Cost
1	2	3	4	5	6
1.	Government of Maharashtra	825.44	–	825.44	19.05
2.	District Council	61.60	–	61.60	1.42
3.	Household Contribution	61.60	–	61.60	1.42
4.	IDA	2648.80	736.12	3384.92	78.11
5.	Total Project Costs	3597.44	736.12	4333.56	100.00

Note: One US Dollar has been converted as Rs. 30.80

TABLE 2.15
Estimate Disbursement

(Annual in Million Rupees)

Sl. No.	IDA Financial Year	1992	1993	1994	1995	1996	1997	1998
1	2	3	4	5	6	7	8	9
1.	Annual	465.08	591.36	766.92	736.12	560.56	258.72	6.16
2.	Cumulative	465.08	1056.44	1823.36	2559.48	3120.04	3378.76	3384.92

Note: (i) Economic Rate of Return (ERR) not applicable.
(ii) One US Dollar has been converted as Rs. 30.80.

The total project cost has been estimated as Rs 43.33 crores, out of which the financial contribution from local sources accounts for Rs. 35.97 crores (83.00%) and foreign sources Rs. 7.36 crores (17.00%). The local sources in percentages as financial contribution comprises of Government of Maharashtra 19.05 per cent, District Council 1.42 per cent, Household contribution 1.42 per cent. The International Development Agencies 61.12 per cent and other foreign sources 17.00 per cent. In other words, the State, local governments and households contribution account for about Rs.9.49 crores or 22 per cent and that of IDA and foreign sources Rs. 33.85 crores or 78 per cent. Further, out of the total Project Costs of Rs 43.34 crores, the Total Base Costs of Rs. 39.12 crores (90.26%) excluding allocation to physical contingencies of Rs 2.77 crores (6.40%) and to price contingencies of Rs 1.45 crores (3.34%) have been assessed for different nine components of the project. In order of priorities, out of nine components of the project, importance in allocation of funds have been accorded to Rural Water Supply Schemes (61.19%), MBSSB Engineering costs (9.88%), Sanitation Programme (6.61%), Institution Building (3.84%), Health Communication (3.69%). Increment of staff salaries (3.20%), Project Support (1.21%), other consultant services (0.50%) and land acquisition (0.14%). (See Tables 2.13 and 2.14).

The estimated amount of Rs. 33.85 crores or 78 per cent to be procured from foreign and IDA sources have also been assessed for disbursement annually/cumulatively from 1992 to 1998 (see Table 2.15).

Conclusion

Maharashtra is one of the prominent States engaged in tackling rural sanitation and drinking water problem in close partnership with Panchayati Raj Institutions. Zilla Parishads occupy a pivotal position in tackling these problems.

C. WORLD HEALTH ORGANIZATION

Introduction

Two decades have passed since the Alma-Ata conference adopted a resolution in 1978 for implementation of Health For All (HFA) by all member states by the year 2000. It is opportune that we evaluate successes and failures of health measures in India, as we are now on the threshold of the 21st Century.

The resolution contained eight components to ensure primary health care to the people as follows:

1. Education on health problems, their prevention;
2. Adequate food supply and proper nutrition;
3. Safe water supply and basic sanitation;
4. Maternal and child health care, and family planning;
5. Universal immunisation;
6. Treatment of common ailment;
7. Prevention and treatment of endemic diseases; and
8. Provision of essential drugs.

Since 1978 onwards, the concept of sanitation has changed considerably. It not only includes personal and domestic hygiene but also food hygiene, safe water supply; disposal of human excreta, waste water and solid waste. The Government of India has already initiated various programmes in the health sector with the partnership of WHO and UNICEF to achieve the goal of "Health For All (HFA) by 2000". Efforts have been made to provide sanitary facilities to prevent diseases and vicious health problems emanating from insanitary conditions prevailing in different areas of the country.

Undoubtedly, we have achieved some progress in the implementation of health care services as evident from the decline in Infant Mortality Rate (IMR) from 144 in 1960 to 77 in 1995 and overall decrease in death rate and increase in life expectancy along with changing patterns of morbidity and mortality. Also, effective and reasonable efforts made to eradicate polio, leprosy and guineaworm diseases as well as reduction in diphtheria, whooping cough, neonatal tetanus and measles deaths, are other remarkable achievements.

But these changes in the process of epidemiological transition are offset by other infectious diseases caused due to deterioration in environmental sanitation levels, such as diarrhoea, acute respiratory infections and malaria; and also non-communicable diseases such as cardiovascular diseases, cancer, diabetes, congenital anomalies, endocrine disorders and accidents, which are causing further morbidity and mortality.

Moreover, the ever-increasing rate of urbanization and growth of industries have added to the health problems because of overcrowding in urban areas, growth of slums and lack of adequate safe water supply and sanitation as well as other essential and basic health facilities and services. These problems have accentuated environmental degradation and added pressure to the already overburdened public health services. The main cause for added concern is drug-resistant strains of tuberculosis, goriococcal infections, malaria and cholera as also HIV/AIDS infections in epidemic proportion. A public health approach at the local levels in urban and rural areas, e.g., Panchayati Raj institutions, in different sectors is the urgent need to effectively control communicable and non-communicable diseases.

Conclusion

Priority issues which threaten the environment and health status of people, such as water supply, sanitation, population growth, urbanization and industrialization, pollution of air, water and soil; food contamination, physical, chemical and radiation hazards and the effects of climatic changes have to be effectively and persuasively implemented and monitored by local bodies in rural and urban areas in collaboration with the Community Based Organisations (CBOs) and Non-governmental organizations (NGOs). This might have salutary impact on environment and health status of the people.

Table 2.16 provides a health status profile based on the data compiled from several sources such as national health bulletins and official publications of the Ministry of Health, Government of India, WHO and other UN agencies and technical units in the South-East Asia Regional Office of WHO.

TABLE 2.16

Demographic, Socio-Economic, Health and Nutrition, Primary Health Care and Gender Equity Indicators

Demographic Indicators	Year	India
Total population (in thousand)	1996	944,580
Surface area (thousands of sq. km)	1994	3,288
Population density (persons per sq. km)	1996	287
Population growth (%)	1990-95	1.91
Crude birth rate (per 1000 populations)	1990-95	29.1
Crude death rate (per 1000 population)	1990-95	10.0
Urban population (%)	1995	26.8
Average annual growth rate of the urban population (%)	1990-95	2.87

Socio-economic Indicators		Year	India
GNP per capita (US $)		1995	340
Average annual growth rate of GNP (%)		1985-95	3.2
Average annual rate of inflation(%)		1985-95	9.8
Human development index		1994	0.45
Dependency ratio:	Total	1995	66.1
	Old-age	1995	7.6
	Young	1995	58.5
Adult literacy rate	Total	1995	52.0
	Female	1995	37.7
	Male	1995	65.5
Gross primary school enrollment ratio (%)			
	Female	1992	89
	Male	1992	112
Gross secondary school enrollment ratio (%)			
	Female	1992	37
	Male	1992	60

TABLE 2.16 *(Contd.)*

Health and Nutrition Indicators		Year	India
Life expectancy at birth (years)	Total	1995	61.1
	Female	1995	61.7
	Male	1995	60.6
Infant mortality rate (per 1000 live births)		1995	74
Under-five mortality rate (per 1000 live births)		1995	n/r
Total fertility rate (per woman)		1990-95	3.75
Maternal mortality ratio (per 100,000 live births)		1995	420
Low-birth-weight new born (%)		1995	30
Children with acceptable weight-for-age (%)		1995	46.6

Primary Health Care Coverage Indicators		Year	India
Infants immunised (%)	DPT3	1995	90
	OPV 3	1995	91
	BCG	1995	96
	Measles	1995	81
Pregnant women immunized with tetanus toxoid (%)		1995	77
Attended by trained personnel (% of live births)			
Pregnant women		1995	85.8
Deliveries		1995	87.1
			43.5
Women of child-bearing age using contraceptive (%)		1995	40.6
Population with access to safe water			
	Total	1995	n/r
	Urban	1995	84.3
	Rural	1995	82.4
Population with access to adequate sanitation			
	Total	1995	n/r
	Urban	1995	49.9
	Rural	1995	3.7

TABLE 2.16 *(Contd.)*

Gender Equity Indicators	Year	India
Gender related development index	1994	0.419
Gender empowerment measure	1994	0.228
Share of earned income (% women)	1994	26
Seats held in parliament (% women)	1996	7.3
Administrators and managers (% women)	1994	2.3
Adult literacy ratio (females as % of males)	1995	58
Primary school enrollment ratio (females as % of males)	1990-94	81
Secondary school enrollment ratio (females as a % of males)	1990-94	64

Note: n/r indicates not reported

Source: World Health Organization, *Regional Health Report*: 1997, South-East Asia Region, New Delhi 1997, pp. 58 to 63.

Conclusion

It is in this scenario, that the environmental sanitation and primary health care facilities and services have to be provided to the rural community. Proper and effective education in environmental sanitation and health of the village community might be an answer to resolve many of these problems. Efforts of the WHO and UNICEF and the Government at different levels including the Panchayati Raj structure calls for not only promotion of sanitation and health facilities but also effective surveillance and monitoring for healthy living of the rural people.

D. GOVERNMENT OF INDIA ASSISTED PROGRAMMES

8. NATIONAL SCHEME OF LIBERATION AND REHABILITATION OF SCAVENGERS

The Ministry of Social Justice and Empowerment is the nodal agency for the scheme. The National Scheme of Liberation and Rehabilitation of Scavengers was launched in March 1992 in pursuance of the Government's commitment to eliminate the inhuman practice of manual handling of night-soil and filth by the end of the Eighth Plan period. The scheme had a time-bound programme for identification of scavengers and their aptitude for alternative occupations through a rapid survey conducted by the District Magistrates/Deputy Commissioners, Urban local bodies and other agencies such as the State Scheduled Caste Development Corporations.

Implementing Agencies

The State Scheduled Caste Development Corporations were designated as the nodal agency for the implementation of the scheme at the grassroots level. The National Scheduled Caste and Scheduled Tribe Finance and Development Corporation (NSFDC) was given the responsibility of day-to-day implementation and monitoring of the scheme as well as the task of coordination and collaboration with the State SCDCs in implementing the scheme. The District Collectors/Deputy Commissioners were made responsible for overall implementation of the scheme. The State governments were expected to identify the training institutes of Central, State and Semi-Governmental organisations where training in different trades would be provided to the intended beneficiaries.

Financial Assistance

The rehabilitation of scavengers in alternative trades was to be achieved by providing a package of financial assistance upto a maximum of Rs. 50,000 per beneficiary. The capital subsidy amounts to Rs. 10,000 or 50 per cent of the capital cost. The other items being, margin money loan of 15 per cent of the project cost at concessional 5 per cent rate of interest and loans from commercial banks for the remaining part under the priority sector lending programme which also carry concessional rates of interest for different slabs of borrowings. An amount of Rs. 50.50 crores in 1991-92, Rs. 60.73 crores in 1992-93 and Rs. 70.97 crores in 1993-94 were released as Central assistance to the State governments. The Plan provision for 1994-95 was Rs. 73 crores out of which Rs. 46.91 crores had been released to the State governments till December 1994 (Annexure-III).

Identification, Training and Rehabilitation

The statewise number of scavengers identified, the progress on training and rehabilitation during the years 1992-93, 1993-94 and 1994-95 are given in Annexure-IV.

A total number of 37,694 scavengers were trained in various trades during the years 1992-93 and 1993-94. The training has been imparted in schemes which include among others, knitting, tailoring, embroidery, typing and shorthand, dairying and other related fields. Some State governments have taken the initiative to train the beneficiaries to become carpenters, blacksmiths, electricians, etc. In addition, 60,863 scavengers were rehabilitated during the same period in the trades mentioned above and other alternative occupations.

National Commission for Safai Karamcharis

The National Commission for Safai Karamcharis started functioning from 12th August, 1994. The Commission would recommend to the Central Government specific programmes for elimination of inequalities in status, facilities and opportunities for safai karamcharis under a time-bound action plan. It would also study and evaluate the programmes and schemes relating to the socio-economic rehabilitation of safai karamcharis.

[*Source:* Government of India, Ministry of Welfare, Annual Report, 1994-95]

Conclusion

Complete elimination of scavenging by the end of the Eighth Plan was one of the national objectives. To attain this commitment, the National Scheme of Liberation and Rehabilitation of scavengers was launched in March 1992. The Ministry of Welfare, Government of India sponsored a research study to evaluate the effectiveness of training and rehabilitation programmes as well as to ascertain the organisational and managerial problems faced in the implementation of the National Scheme. The Evaluation study was conducted by the Council for Social Development, New Delhi during 1994, in two towns, namely Meerut and Allahabad in Uttar Pradesh.

Some of the major findings of the Evaluation Study are noteworthy.

(i) 27.3 per cent of the sample population in Meerut and 25.2 per cent in Allahabad are still engaged in scavenging.
(ii) A large number of dry latrines still exist in both the towns;
(iii) As many as 31.8 per cent in Allahabad and 17.2 per cent in Meerut were rehabilitated as sweepers in municipal corporations;
(iv) On completion of training 37.5 per cent of the scavengers in Meerut and 47.0 per cent in Allahabad were self-employed . . . majority of the respondents expressed that duration of training may be increased;
(v) There seems to be lack of awareness about the scheme among the members of the implementing agencies for which a short training programme may be arranged;
(vi) There is an absence of positive linkage between executing agency and the community to initiate the process for effective and complete rehabilitation, not mere alternate occupation of a temporary nature, and
(vii) Though the list of identified trades covers a wide range, many of the trades lack relevance to the needs of the communities at large, particularly women and children. It is suggested that areas of vocations and fields of training need to be indicated enabling flexibility for careful adoption of programmes to suit local conditions.

E. SULABH INTERNATIONAL SOCIAL SERVICE ORGANIZATION (SISSO) ASSISTED PROGRAMMES

Sulabh International Social Service Organization (SISSO) a Non-Governmental Organization of repute (henceforward will be referred to in this study as Sulabh) founded by Dr. Bindeshwar Pathak, a man of determined will and vision, launched various projects in different areas of the country on Environmental Sanitation and Health sectors for promoting integrated rural development. It has evolved alternate options for intervention based on the application of Sulabh Concept and Objectives respecting traditional values and cultural ethos of the people of different areas in tune with appropriate scientific and technological inputs. The methodology and operational strategies of Sulabh action programmes thus vary in different regions according to aspirations and the needs of the people in terms of priorities, which emerge basically from people's initiative and participation at the grassroots level.

At the outset, it may be stated that it is reported that the SISSO has not sought any financial support from outside sources for implementing different models, but has implemented them either through its own funds or those raised from the people or grants from State governments or other institutions after getting requisite approval.

Concept

The basic concept of Model villages for integrated rural development propounded by Sulabh, not only envisages making available to each household and the village community, appropriate sanitation and health facilities, but also seeks to arouse amongst the people an awareness about the inter-relationship and mutual dependence of economic factors affecting options for sanitation requirements. The guiding principle of the concept is to place people at the centre stage of development by ensuring retention of traditional values and integrating those with appropriate modern technology, affordable and acceptable to the village community. The process to achieve these include sensitising the people through information, education and communication (IEC) methods as well as sustained awareness and motivation campaigns. This is done mainly to restore the right of the people and the village community to take decisions for their healthy and fruitful living in rural environment.

Objectives

The main objectives of the Model village for integrated rural development are:

(i) To assess the existing and potential physical, human and financial resources of the area;

(ii) To prepare 'Action Plan' for providing improved environmental sanitation and health education at the household and community levels primarily through different panchayat institutions;

(iii) To ensure better living conditions at the household and community levels by providing low-cost sanitation and health facilities, safe-drinking water, safe disposal of solid and liquid wastes, through appropriate technology,

(iv) To help 'Panchayat Institutions' establish inter-sectoral linkages for increased employment and income-generation activities for equitable and sustainable rural development.

Methodology and Operational Strategies

The broad spectrum of methodology and operational strategies has been spelled out in the Sulabh integrated rural development programmes, with adequate in-built provisions for changes after assessing the situation in project areas and the people's aspirations and needs in terms of priorities. They are as follows:

(i) To conduct bench-mark socio-economic survey of the village in order to assess the existing status of physical, human and financial resources,

(ii) To sensitise the rural community after making them aware about their resources in order to tap their strength of self-reliance and introduce measures to overcome weaknesses emanating from ignorance, inertia, poverty and unemployment etc.;

(iii) To help panchayat institutions in 'Planning and implementation through their own committees (particularly for women and youths) for effective promotion of development activities and welfare of the people with focus on schools, *anganwadi*, safe-drinking water, sanitation, health, infrastructure development viz., road, electricity, biogas etc.,

(iv) To assess health status of each individual of the village and organise preventive and curative measures emphasising the importance of Integral System of Yoga, Ayurvedic, Herbal and Allopathic treatment; as and when required;

(v) To provide low-cost sanitary latrines and safe-drinking water facilities to each household; and

(vi) To help panchayat institutions in setting up of cottage and small-scale industries for utilization of local resources to promote employment and income-generation activities.

9. HARYANA

Experimental Rural Sanitation Programme

Based on the Concept and Objectives formulated by the Sulabh (SISSO) for promoting environment-friendly integrated rural development programmes, an attempt was made in five villages (viz., Bhondsi, Teekli, Palara, Akleempur and Naya Gaon) of Sohna block in Gurgaon district, Haryana. Briefly, the physical and demographic features of Gurgaon district, where the five villages in Sohna block are situated are explained hereunder.

Gurgaon District

Gurgaon district covers an area of 2760 sq. kms. The total population of the district was 11.5 lakhs comprising 6.2 lakhs males and 5.3 lakhs females, as per 1991 Census. The rural population of 9.1 lakhs and urban population of 2.4 lakhs clearly indicate the relevance of rural development and dependence on agriculture. This is exemplified by the net area sown i.e. 1930 sq. kms. One of the notable characteristics of the district is the establishment of many large-scale industries in the recent past such as Maruti Udyog Ltd., Kelvinator India Ltd, Carrier Aircon Ltd., Munjal Showa Ltd., Bharat Seats Ltd, etc. The level of urbanization of 20.30 per cent in the district is below the State average of 24.63 per cent and All-India level of 25.73 per cent. Another significant feature of the district is the literacy rate of 52.61 per cent, a little above the All-India rate of 52.21

per cent but lower than that of the State level of 55.85 per cent. Further, it is a very encouraging feature that the male literacy rate of the district is 67.87 per cent, above the All-India average of 64.13 per cent, but lower than that of the State literacy rate of 69.10 per cent. On the other hand, it is disheartening to note that the female literacy rate of 23.45 per cent is far below the All-India rate of 39.29 per cent and State rate of 25.31 per cent. Moreover, the rural literacy rate of 34.96 per cent is also far below the All-India rate of 44.69 per cent and that of State rate of 36.66 per cent.

Demonstration Programme

The Sulabh initiated an experimental project to implement construction of Two-Pit Pour-Flush latrines in 100 households of five villages in order to judge the effectiveness of this facility and people's response in this regard. The details are noted below:

TABLE 2.17
Sulabh Demonstration Programme in Gurgaon District

Village	Population		No. of Families		No. of P.F latrine constructed
	1981	1991	1981	1991	
Bhondsi	4731	7738	1600	N.A	14
Teekli	3539	4577	900	1006*	67
Palara	1706	2634	400	N.A	5
Akleempur	656	1147	200	N.A	13
Naya Gaon	–	–	250	N.A	1
					100

* As per bench-mark survey

Note: (i) Including Naya Gaon Hamlet population included in Bhondsi population of 1981 and 1991 census.

(ii) All are revenue villages.

All the selected villages are located between 11 km and 16 km from Gurgaon on Gurgaon-Sohna-Jaipur road. The physical survey of these villages revealed that they are in a hilly-terrain having sandy-loam soil with scanty rainfall. It was also found that none of these villages had ever any dry or bucket latrines. Few households possessed septic-tank latrines. A majority of the people, including women and children, have all through been defecating in the open field. They were quite ignorant about low-cost sanitation technology. An awareness campaign for adoption of this technology was launched. The selection of beneficiaries in these villages was on the basis of their willingness for installation of Pour Flush latrines in their households. To make it a financially viable proposition, M/s Modi Industries Ltd. was requested to collaborate for achieving the target of 100 units of household latrines. It was an encouraging experience, when M/s Modi Industries Ltd. ventured to contribute Rs. 2,000 for construction of one unit of sanitary latrine in rural area. The estimated cost of construction of different sizes and specification of a unit Pour Flush latrine varied between Rs. 1707 and Rs. 3860. The type of Pour Flush latrine depended on the preference and paying capacity of beneficiaries which included the grant amount of Rs. 2,000 per unit contributed by M/s Modi Industries Ltd.

The whole programme was implemented within a period of three to four months. The participation of the beneficiaries in getting P.F. latrines installed in their households had a demonstration impact through which the effectiveness of the programme and the extent of affordability of different categories and classes of beneficiaries was assessed. This experimental programme achieved success with the efforts of dedicated social workers and technical personnel of the Sulabh (SISSO). It was implemented and monitored by them with due precision for its use and maintenance for over a year or so. After an in-depth enquiry, it was revealed that there has been total acceptance and adoption of the low-cost sanitation programme and technology in a tradition-bound rural society. This experimental programme had a salutary effect amongst the people and they were encouraged to have atleast a sanitary latrine *inter alia* to enhance their social status.

Teekli Village Model

The demonstration impact of experimental programme of low-cost sanitation in five villages of Sohna Block in Gurgaon district, encouraged the people of Teekli village to take up other rural development programmes for overall prosperity of the village community. Teekli was selected for development as a Model village for three obvious reasons. First, the receptivity of the people for adoption of technological innovations for social change; second, the perception and initiative of the people to participate in the rural development programmes under the leadership of the Pradhan of Teekli Village Panchayat Samiti and its members; and third, the catalyst role played by the social workers and functionaries of Sulabh in formulating an Action Plan for the Model Village: Teekli helped the Panchayat Samiti and the people to decide the prioritization of development needs after a series of meetings and consultations with the people and members of the Panchayat Samiti. The programme for the Model village, Teekli was initiated on July 23, 1994.

Resource Inventory and Socio-Economic Survey

The physical resource inventory and socio-economic survey of Teekli village was conducted by the Sulabh Institute of Rural Development (SIRD) and the Sulabh International Institute of Health and Hygiene (SIIHH) in order to understand and explain to the people different options for the possible activities to be undertaken for optimum utilization of physical, human and financial resources.

The survey indicated that Teekli village covers a total area of 370.66 sq. acres. It is situated on alluvial plain surrounded by mountain terrain. The alluvial formation is mixed up with sandy loam and claystone soil. The surface water table ranges between 18.90 metres and 19.81 metres. There is scanty rainfall in the area. But lack of drainage system creates problems of sanitation on roads and lanes of the village due to spilled-over water released from each household. Piped water supply is available in some houses. There are 412 Tubewells and water released through them is fit for irrigation and drinking purposes.

The benchmark socio-economic survey conducted during

April 1994 by the SIRD indicated that the total population of 4,577 as per 1991 Census increased to 4,859 persons, which comprises 2,629 males and 2,230 females. There are 1,006 families in the village living in 631 households and hence the average size of family works out to 4.8, which is lower than the national average of 5.2 per family.

The total number of animals is 1,014 viz., buffaloes 684 (68%), cows 202 (20%) and others 128 which includes bullock, camels and pigs etc. (12%). The dung and urine of animals are considered as a superior quality bio-fertilizer. This may also be used for various purposes by linking agriculture with animal husbandry, and also for bio-energy production in order to improve environmental sanitation and health status of the people.

There are different types of trees, such as Shisham, Banana, *Enavas arabica*, Gular Pras, Berry, Pomegranate, Lrisoda, available in the village. 'Tulsi' plants and Neem trees are very effective to cure many diseases. The project has assessed all these resources in order to promote herbal treatment and use of such plants as a preventive measure to health hazards.

The village has a composite population. Out of 631 households, there are 461 Yadav families (73%) followed by 136 Scheduled Caste families (22%) and the rest 34 (5%) belong to either Backward Classes, or are goldsmiths, barbers, khati and brahman.

There are five schools in the village, Government High School, Primary Girl's School, Shiksha Bharti, Shree Chitragupta Public School and Sharma Public School. There are 51 teachers in these schools having 1,468 students in different classes. Out of 4,859 persons in the village, the number of literate persons is 2,590 (53.3%) and illiterate persons 2,269 (46.7%). Among the literate persons (2590), it is reported that 652 persons are having higher educational levels (upto high school 475, intermediate 82, graduate 73, post-graduate 15, doctor 2, engineer and other technical persons 5 only) and the remaining 1948 are literate but do not have higher educational levels. It seems that the level of education is good but the level of illiteracy is also high. It is amongst these people that an awareness has to be created for participation in the process of social and economic development.

Methodology and Operational Strategy

For the implementation of programme in the village Teekli, an 'Action Plan' was prepared in July 1994 by the Sulabh in consultation with the Pradhan, members of the Panchayat Samiti and the people of the village. The status of the physical and human resource endowment was explained, and thereafter prioritization of activities to be undertaken and institutional committees to be constituted for carrying out the programmes for different activities was discussed and finalized.

It may be noted that among all the activities to be undertaken such as health, sanitation, infrastructure facilities like safe drinking water, road, drainage, solid and water waste management, small-scale and cottage industries for employment and income-generation, it was the unanimous decision of the people to choose the 'Health status' of the people as an 'entry point' for understanding the need for not only sanitation and safe drinking water facilities to be provided at household and community level but also for composite development of the whole village after optimum utilization of physical and human resources.

Achievements

Different committees have been constituted to achieve the above objectives in collaboration with the functionaries of the Sulabh International Social Service Organisation.

Institutional Committees

(i) *Panchayat Samiti Development Committee*

This Committee is headed by Pradhan, having 14 active members of the Panchayat Samiti. The Development Committee looks after the overall development of the village community by constituting different "Beneficiary and Scheme committees", which works and collaborates with the functionaries of the Sulabh; procures funds from the government and the people; and identifies trained resource persons from the village and/or impart training to the people from the village or even outside to accelerate the process of development activities. So far 21 trained youths in the village have been identified who are technically qualified but still awaiting fruitful employment opportunities. A library has been set up by Sulabh in Panchayat Bhawan.

(ii) *Anganwadi Committees*

The village has been divided into five zones and five Anganwadi Committees have been formed to look after the health and welfare of children below 5 years and the health status of their mothers. These Anganwadi zones cover health programmes concerned with immunization, family planning, prenatal and antinatal care, nutritional status of each person and educates people on health and sanitation aspects.

(iii) *Women's Welfare Society*

The Society has been registered, which comprise 13 women members of the village to look after the welfare of women from all aspects.

(iv) *Students Kalyan Samiti*

The Students, Teachers and Parents' Committees has been formed in all the five schools of the village to promote health and sanitation education as well as to impart training in Yoga practices and to provide herbal treatment. The students are also given training to follow these practices and also to improve their nutrition status by planting trees and cultivating vegetables near their households and school gardens. Sulabh Sports Club has been formed, where students from all the five schools take active part in the games like volleyball, cricket, etc. Sulabh has renovated a student toilet complex in Government High School with the contribution made by parent-teachers' association. Now both the teachers and students use and maintain this complex.

Health and Sanitation for Environmental Upgradation

In terms of priority, Health Sector was considered by the

Panchayat Samiti Development Committee to be an initiator for development activities in the Model village, Teekli.

The Sulabh International Institute of Health and Hygiene (SIIHH) designed Family Medical Folder/Cards for Health Check-up of each member of the household as well as to find out the diseases and health hazards emanating from insanitary conditions. The folders/cards designed are as follows:
Family Medical Folder of Health Care contains:

(i) Sulabh Health Check-Up Card of each household
(ii) Sulabh Postnatal Check-Up Card : Mother
(iii) Sulabh Antinatal Check -Up Card : Mother
(iv) Sulabh Health Check-Up Card of each child of the household with immunisation schedule
(v) Guidelines Card for immunization
(vi) Medical Identity Card of Blood Donors with Blood Groups and R.H. Factor.

Achievement in Health Sector

With the filling up of these cards, the health status of every person has been assessed. The preventive and curative measures have also been initiated.

In particular, the Health Unit of the SIIHH completed the following:

- Prepared the Family Health Records of all the 1,006 families (100%)
- Medical check-up of 3,920 (85%) families
- Prenatal check-up of all the pregnant women (100%)
- Immunization/vaccination of 989 children (below 5 years)
- Vaccination of 646 persons (above 5 years)
- Complete Medical check-up of all students (100%)
- Blood check-up (Blood group and R.H Factor) of 150 voluntary blood donors
- Persons identified for Family Planning Operations
- Eye Problems identified and being treated.

It is reported that due to 100 per cent coverage under

immunization programme to new-born children and children below 5 years, there has been significant decline in the incidence of diseases like tetanus, diphtheria, whooping cough, measles and tuberculosis. Further, there has also been decline in the case of diarrhoea and gastro-intestinal diseases (particularly intestinal worms etc.) due to adoption of sanitation and health measures. It is observed that the traditional taboos and habits of the people have changed to a reasonable extent due to health and sanitation education and awareness created by Sulabh.

Sanitation, Safe Drinking Water Supply and other Development Programmes

After assessing the health status, the proposal of the Panchayat Samiti Development Committee has been to take up sanitation, safe-water supply and other development programmes as follows.

(i) Low-cost sanitary latrines: As stated earlier, 67 Pour Flush latrines were installed during experimental project of SISSO and thereafter 232 P.F. latrines have been constructed with government subsidy and people's contribution. The remaining 332 P.F. latrines is likely to be installed. For this the Panchayat Samiti Development Committee and the SIRD have initiated efforts to procure funds from the government and the village community so that this 'Model village' may be proclaimed as a "Whole Village Approach" having Pour Flush latrine in each household.

(ii) "Dust-Bin" has been designed by the Sulabh so that each household may keep the waste material of the house which will be collected in 'closed cycle-rickshaw or bullock-cart' to be dumped at the specified place in village or near the bio-gas plants to be utilized as recycling waste products for generation of bio-energy.

(iii) Five bio-gas plants which are non-functional are proposed to be made functional for utilization of energy for the proposed Small-Scale Tile industry. The Panchayat Samiti has also initiated to set up cottage industries of Mustard grinding plant, as well as Sarkand's chair and Munz baskets. It is reported that the resources for setting up these cottage industries are available in this village. People in the village have been identified for training. Marketing of these products has been thought over. Profit of these industries will be shared by the people and the Panchayat Samiti.

(iv) Panchayat Samiti has proposed to provide safe drinking water through piped water supply to a large number of houses for which action is being taken by the Panchayat Samiti and the Sulabh.

(v) The most important priority of the village community is levelling and construction of 'Pucca Road' in the village, the estimated cost of which is about Rs. 25 lakhs as worked out by the SISSO/SIRD and placed before the Panchayat Samiti Development Committee.

(vi) The project has planned the Yoga training to be introduced particularly amongst the children of the village schools and also amongst the adults of the village community along with the training to use herbal plants as a traditional method to keep everyone fit and healthy. Training is also proposed to be given to school children to grow nutritious plants in their kitchen gardens/schools.

Conclusion

The prominent feature of Teekli village model evolved by the Sulabh is the involvement of Panchayat Institutions in tackling sanitation and health problems through general application of socio-economic development of the village as a whole with unbiased support of a Non-Governmental Organisation. Though the experiment is in its infancy, it has the potential to be a viable model, if handled with imagination, care, dedication and people's understanding.

10. ORISSA

Ganjam and Puri: District Model

The total population of Orissa is 315 lakhs comprising of 160 lakhs males and 155 lakhs females as per 1991 Census. There are 30 districts, 314 blocks, (including 114 tribal blocks) and 50,972 villages in the State of Orissa. The literacy rate of 34.12 per cent in the State is far below the All-India average literacy rate of 52.21 per cent.

During 1983-84, the State government in collaboration with UNICEF carried out Rural Sanitation Programme in 25 villages of 5 blocks to construct 2,250 household latrines and 13 school latrines as post-flood rehabilitation programme. In 1986-88, the State government collaborated with UNICEF for construction of 9,630 household latrines in 15 I.C.D.S blocks. Further, the UNICEF collaborated with the State government in the 'Golden Triangle Project' in revenue villages of 12 blocks to construct household latrines, anganwadi latrines and primary health centre latrines with a view to prevent road side defecation from Bhubaneswar to Konark, Konark to Puri, and Puri to Bhubaneswar route. These roads form a triangle and most of the tourist spots are situated along these roads. It is reported that the objective of the project was to prevent environmental pollution to promote tourism but has not achieved the desired objective, because the practice of road-side defecation around the Golden Triangle could not be curbed.

The State government also got household latrines constructed in many blocks under RLEGP and CRSP programmes of the Ministry of Rural Development (now Ministry of Rural Areas and Employment), Government of India. Besides, these efforts, the State government collaborated with DANIDA, in rural sanitation programme in 5 blocks of 3 districts (Puri, Cuttack and Balasore) to construct 2,954 household latrines.

These random, piecemeal efforts in regard to Rural Sanitation Programmes were not an adequate answer as the magnitude of the problems involved was very large. The Department of Rural Development of the State government, therefore, entrusted to Sulabh for the preparation of a feasibility report of Ganjam and Puri districts, which may be considered as a model for launching massive programmes for construction of household latrines and community complexes in rural areas of the State. This was prompted, firstly, keeping in view the track record of Sulabh's contribution in Urban Sanitation Programme. Sulabh had constructed 19,292 household latrines out of 21,429 in 74 local bodies (out of 102 urban local bodies) and 114 community complexes in 35 local bodies. Secondly, after assessing Sulabh's contribution in construction of Rural Community Complexes, which are operated and maintained properly from 1989-90 onwards (This will be discussed in the later part of this section of the study).

The basic features of Ganjam and Puri districts may be seen in the Table 2.18. It indicates that the rural population in Ganjam and Puri districts is 2.69 lakhs and 2.88 lakhs, respectively. The male and female population in both the districts represents more or less the same ratio. The rate of urbanisation of 19.67 per cent in Puri district is above the State average rate of 13.38 per cent and below the national average rate of 25.73 per cent. On the other hand, the rate of urbanization of 14.90 per cent in Ganjam district is not only below Puri district but also far below the national average of 25.73 per cent and a little above the State average of 13.38 per cent.

TABLE 2.18

Basic Features of Ganjam and Puri Districts

(1991 Census)

Indicators		Ganjam	Puri
Total Area (sq. kms)		12531	10162
Total Population (Lakhs)		3.16	3.59
Male "		1.57	1.85
Female "		1.59	1.74
Urban "		0.47	0.71
Rural "		2.69	2.88
Urbanisation	(%)	14.90	19.67
Literacy	(%)	44.26	63.82
Male "	(%)	60.77	76.82
Female "	(%)	28.09	49.94
Urban "	(%)	68.82	78.60
Rural "	(%)	39.79	60.11

The literacy rate of 63.82 per cent in Puri district is far above the State rate of 49.09 per cent and also the national rate of 52.21. It indicates that the rural population in Puri district having 60.11 per cent of literacy rate may be considered to be quite receptive to rural development programmes through proper awareness and motivation campaign. Whereas in Ganjam district, the rural literacy rate of 39.79 per cent is not only far below the Puri district but also the State and national literacy rates of 45.46 per cent and 44.69 per cent respectively.

There are four major industrial units in Puri district, viz., Amalgam Foods Ltd., Dharani Sugars and Chemicals Ltd., Alsa Marine and Harvests Ltd., and Ferro Alloys Corporation Ltd. In Ganjam district, there are only two major industrial units viz., Jayshree Chemicals Ltd. and India Rare Earths Ltd. Besides, there are large number of small-scale industries, which provide employment opportunity to the people.

It is in the above scenario, that the rural sanitation programme has to be viewed. A socio-economic sample survey was conducted by the Sulabh (SISSO) in five representative blocks of both Ganjam and Puri districts covering 10 villages and 300 households in each district in order to assess the felt need of the rural community about sanitary latrines as well as their willingness to participate in latrine construction and their capacity for financial contribution. The findings of the survey reveal that in Ganjam district all the interviewed households expressed their willingness to have sanitary latrines in their household, whereas in Puri district 76.6 per cent expressed their willingness to install sanitary latrines and 23.4 per cent still preferred to defecate in the open. The capacity of beneficiaries to repay loan in monthly instalments varied between Rs. 20 and Rs. 50 only. In Puri district 91.9 per cent were willing to pay Rs. 20 per month, and 1.6 per cent Rs. 50 per month whereas in Ganjam district 54.4 per cent were agreeable to pay Rs. 20 per month, 4.6 per cent Rs. 50 and 13.3 per cent households were not in a position to repay the loan. It was also revealed that with reasonable software and institutional support from the government and the implementing agency, an NGO, could boost the programme.

The Model has been structured by Sulabh (SISSO) for launching the Rural Sanitation Programme in both districts with detailed guidelines. The steps to be taken up in terms of:

(i) *Implementation Strategy and Procedure*

(a) Size of the programme
(b) Financing patterns
(c) Selection of villages
(d) Selection of beneficiaries
(e) Health education and motivation
(f) Construction of demonstration latrines
(g) Feedback results
(h) Modification of the programme

(ii) *Construction Methodology*

(a) Application for latrines
(b) Signing of the agreement
(c) Actual construction
(d) Participation of the people in latrine construction

Further, the Model, also describes the technology of Pour-Flush Latrines in terms of its merits and suitability; its water requirement; component parts; leach pits; inspection chamber; footrest; flooring pit covers etc. Besides, the Model prescribes five types of tested designs with specification of sanitary latrines, the estimated cost of which ranges between Rs. 2,275 and Rs. 4,750 and which could be installed in the project district in the households of beneficiaries in terms of their preferences and paying capacity.

The Model works out the estimated total cost of construction of five different types of rural sanitary latrines aiming at covering from 10 per cent to 100 per cent in a phased manner. It also suggests as to how funds could be procured from HUDCO for different categories of beneficiaries to meet the estimated cost of the project.

Rural Community Complexes

In order to promote Rural Sanitation Programme, the Community Development and Rural Construction (CDRC)

Department of the Government of Orissa selected Sulabh International Social Service Organisation (SISSO) for construction of 8 rural community complexes in 1989-90, mainly near prominent temples in six districts of the State. The total cost of construction was Rs. 22.15 lakhs. This created an impact and the State government again selected Sulabh in 1991-92 for construction of 12 more rural community complexes at 12 important locations in Ganjam district alone. The total cost of construction amounted to Rs 66.00 lakhs only. In view of popularity of these complexes in rural areas, the State government approached the Sulabh in 1992-93, for construction of 26 rural community complexes at important locations such as District and Sub-Divisional Headquarters in many districts of the State. The total cost of these complexes was Rs. 150 lakhs. Thus between 1989-90 and 1992-93, the Sulabh has constructed 46 rural community complexes at different important rural locations at a total cost of Rs. 238.15 lakhs.

All these rural community complexes are self-sustainable on "pay and use" system. These complexes are well maintained by the Sulabh and each Community Complex has 10 seats latrine facility (7 for males and 3 for females). They also have bathing cubicles (5 for men and 3 for women). These complexes have been installed with independent water supply through deep Tubewells with lift pumps of one and a half horsepower.

Assessment

The Sulabh International Social Service Organisation (SISSO) has been the most notable NGO involved in implementation of low cost sanitation (conversion and construction activities) in both rural and urban areas of Orissa. Recently, some NGOs have also been involved in implementation of low cost sanitation activities, particularly construction of low cost household latrines in rural areas as shown in Table 2.19.

TABLE 2.19
Household Latrines under Rural Sanitation Programme constructed by different NGOs in Orissa (1994-97)

Sl.	Name of NGOs	No. of Latrines
1.	OREDA, Bhubaneswar	9962
2.	FARR, Dhenkanal	5247
3.	UAA, Ganjam	5542
4.	CYSD, Bhubaneswar	5253
5.	Banabasi	1537
6.	Lokashakti	1478
7.	Sulabh International	2921
8.	ISAAC, Sambalpur	1513
9.	Agragamee	503
10.	BGVS	2755
11.	39 NGOs	465
	Total	37176

Total expenditure Rs. 6,96,82,667 (Rupees six crores ninety six lakhs eighty two thousand six hundred sixty seven only.)
Source: Sulabh International Social Service Organisation, Orissa State Branch, Bhubaneswar.

It is reported that a total of 37,175 individual Household latrines were constructed at a total cost of Rs. 6,96,82,667 (Rupees six crores ninety six lakhs eighty two thousand six hundred sixty seven only, during 1994-97 by different NGOs including SISSO. Besides construction of Institutional latrines, women complexes, Sulabh Sauchalaya community complexes in both rural and urban areas were undertaken by SISSO. The brief description of each of these activities is as under.

Institutional Latrines

The implementation of Institutional latrines in selected colleges and High schools were taken up under Rural Sanitation Programme. Sulabh International being the only implementing agency completed 406 institutional latrines at a total expenditure of Rs. 67,54,216 (Rupees sixty seven lakhs fifty four thousand two hundred sixteen only) during the year 1994-97.

Women Complexes

During the year 1994-1997, 209 women complexes in selected women's colleges and Girl's High Schools were constructed by Sulabh International at an expenditure of Rs. 34,76,924 (Rupees thirty four lakhs seventy six thousand nine hundred twenty four only). Sulabh International is the only implementing Agency in Orissa for this scheme.

Sulabh Shauchalaya Complexes

Forty-two Sulabh Shauchalaya Complexes at different locations selected by the Rural Development Department were constructed by Sulabh International at an expenditure of Rs. 3,13,15,677 (Rupees three crores thirteen lakhs fifteen thousand six hundred seventy seven only) during the years 1994-97.

Funds were made available by the Rural Development Department of Orissa Government directly to Sulabh International. These are reported to have been completed to the best satisfaction of the Government Authorities.

Urban Areas

Sulabh International is the only implementing agency in Orissa, as per the decision of the State government, for implementation of various types of sanitation schemes. During the period 1994-1997, a total number of 44,012 household latrines under Integrated Scheme of Low Cost Sanitation have been completed by Sulabh International at an expenditure of Rs. 8,35,22,569 (Rupees eight crores thirty five lakhs twenty two thousand five hundred sixty nine only). The number towns covered in this scheme during the period 1994-1997 was 94.

Financing pattern till 1989-90 was 50% from the Government of India, Ministry of Welfare and 50% by the State Government or Urban Local Bodies. From 1990-91 onwards the financing pattern is 45% subsidy from the Ministry of Urban Development, Govt. of India, a 50% loan through HUDCO and 5% beneficiaries contribution.

Sulabh Complexes

A total of 164 Sulabh Complexes have been constructed in 96 towns at an expenditure of Rs. 5,52,82,000 (Rupees five crores fifty two lakhs eighty two thousand only) during the years 1994-1997.

The financing pattern for this scheme is 50% as grant-in-aid from the State government and 50% by the Urban Local Bodies. This scheme, implemented by Sulabh International is operated and maintained by the organisation on 'Pay & Use' basis.

Conclusion

Orissa State has been declared as Scavenging free State because there is no dry latrine in any town. The scavengers (1591) engaged previously in cleaning of dry latrines have been liberated and provided alternative jobs of cleaning roads, buildings and drains by the Urban Local Bodies. The Orissa Scheduled Castes and Scheduled Tribes Development Finance Co-operative Corporation Limited is responsible for providing training to the wards of the scavengers. However, no such programme exclusively for them have been taken up. Funds for training and re-habilitation is available from the Ministry of Welfare, Government of India.

The Sulabh International Social Service Organisation's (SISSO) contribution in promoting low-cost sanitation programme in the urban areas has been applauded by the people. They have accepted the usefulness of household latrines and community complexes. In view of the track record of Sulabh in conversion/construction of household latrines and community complexes in urban and rural areas, the Government of Orissa involved it in the preparation of Ganjam and Puri District Model for rural sanitation programme, and depending upon its success, the organisation might cover the rest of the districts in the State, in due course.

11. BIHAR

Samastipur and Gaya: District Model

The Sulabh Movement initiated by the Sulabh International Social Service Organisation (SISSO) during the early seventies, in urban areas of Bihar, for experimentation and implementation of low-cost multi-dimensional sanitation technology snowballed gradually into the national and international arena. Now the SISSO has launched a movement for utilisation of low-cost sanitation technology for Rural Reconstruction in Bihar by not only conversion/construction of household latrines and community complexes but also implementation of programmes for safe drinking water, solid waste and water management, bio-energy generation and thereby environmental upgradation by optimum mobilization of physical, financial and human resources for integrated rural development.

In Bihar, Samastipur and Gaya districts have been selected by Sulabh. Some of the important features of both the districts have been indicated in Table 2.20

TABLE 2.20

Basic Features of Samastipur and Gaya Districts

(1991 Census)

Indicators		Samastipur	Gaya
Area	sq. kms	2904.00	4976.00
Net Sown Area	"	1848.65	3308.39
Net Irrigated Area	"	605.14	2606.83
Total Population (Lakh)		2.72	2.66
Male	"	1.41	1.38
Female	"	1.31	1.28
Urban	"	0.14	0.35
Rural	"	2.58	2.31
Literacy	(%)	36.37	40.47
Male	"	50.39	55.22
Female	"	21.17	24.20
Urban	"	64.69	70.76
Rural	"	34.83	35.61

It may be seen from Table 2.20 that while the districts of Samastipur and Gaya are having a total population of 2.72 lakh and 2.66 respectively as per 1991 Census, the geographical area varies widely. Consequently, the density of population is lower in Gaya. In Samastipur, 0.21 per cent of land is irrigated whereas in Gaya about 0.52 per cent of land is under irrigation. Maximum concentration of rural population is in Samastipur, where low-cost sanitation facilities are being provided.

Prior to launching any rural development programme, an important prerequisite is the assessment of level of education and literacy amongst the people (male and female) in rural areas, particularly in programme like low-cost sanitation where technological innovation have to be introduced for adoption. Campaign for awareness has chances of greater success when people are literate. The Table 2.20 indicates that the literacy rate of 40.47 per cent in Gaya district is above State literacy rate of 38.48 per cent, but lower than that of national rate of 52.21 per cent, whereas the literacy rate of 36.37 per cent in Samastipur is lower to the State rate and far below the national rate. Male literacy rate in both districts is far above the female literacy as the Table shows. On the other hand, the rural literacy rate is around 35 per cent in both districts, a little above the State rate of about 34 per cent, but far below the national rate of 44.69 per cent.

Samastipur district has three large scale industrial units viz. New India Sugar Mills Ltd., Winsome International Ltd., and Rameshwar Jute Mills Ltd., Besides, there are large number of small-scale industries, which provide employment opportunity to workers in different areas. In Gaya district, there is no major industry, but medium and small scale industries have been established. Both the districts are well connected by road and railways.

Implementation Strategy

It is in the above scenario of physical and human resource endowment, Sulabh Sauchayalaya Sansthan under the auspices of the Sulabh International Social Service Organisation (SISSO) launched initially low-cost sanitation programme under Integrated Rural Development Programmes of the Government in order to assess, firstly, the aspiration of the people and secondly, to create awareness amongst the people for adoption of low-cost sanitation schemes. The implementation of the programme is in nascent stage but gradually taking its root in the rural areas of both districts.

In regard to physical achievement, it is reported that in 22 panchayats of Samastipur block, 47 community latrine complexes have been constructed either of 2, 3 or 4 seats along with one hand pump in each complex at different locations. Thus 47 handpumps have been installed. 42 community complexes have also been installed in Jitwarpur block followed by 3 in Morwa block and one each in Kalyanpur and Mohiuddin Nagar blocks. The special feature of these complexes is that this facility is provided mainly for women under Jawahar Rozgar Yojana. Sulabh has also taken up construction of over 500 household latrines in different panchayats of the district, mainly in Jitwarpur, Bibhutipur, Morwa and Wasinagar blocks under Self-Financing Scheme. It is reported that the Sulabh will cover all the 14 blocks in the district to provide low-cost sanitary latrine, community complexes and safe-drinking water facilities for which 'Action Programme' has been prepared by the Sulabh after assessing the felt need of the people in different villages of 14 blocks in the district.

In Gaya district, the main objective of the low cost sanitation programme is initially: (a) to highlight the need for environmental sanitation, (b) to create mass awareness for the need to preserve the sanctity of environment, and (c) to launch a programme for construction of low cost sanitation latrines and community complexes and baths in all the panchayat institutions of different blocks of the district. It is proposed to cover 500 villages of the district with low-cost sanitation facilities. To create a demonstration impact, over 40 household latrines have been installed in different blocks. Construction of another 15 household latrines is in progress under Self-Financing Scheme. Awareness and motivation campaign have been conducted amongst the people. It is being ensured that flow of funds to the project area for different components of rural sanitation programmes such as low-cost sanitation and handpump for safe drinking water are also released from State Rural Development Department.

Conclusion

Although both the districts of Samastipur and Gaya are in nascent stage of evolving a model, yet it promises to emerge as a viable model, where configuration of efforts would be the prominent component, especially through the efforts of Non-Governmental Organisations.

12. RAJASTHAN

The Rural Sanitation Programme (RSP) is being implemented by the Sanitation Cell at the State level under the Department of Rural Development and Panchayati Raj. The programme is operating in all the 30 districts, out of which UNICEF is assisting in 17 districts. The rural sanitation programme target is to cover 25 per cent families by the turn of the century after providing sanitary facilities at household and institutional level, as well as facility park for women, training centre etc. Although the planning process has been evolved to achieve the target yet much need to be done to cover the entire rural population.

Sulabh International Social Service Organisation (SISSO)

Sulabh was assigned the task of construction/conversion of dry latrines in 1984-85. It is reported that the SISSO converted/ constructed 1,12,866 pour-flush latrines and 221 community complexes (pay and use system) of different sizes in 86 towns in 29 districts of Rajasthan from 1984-85 to March 1995.

In view of the role played by the SISSO in urban areas as well as awareness and motivation created for the effectiveness of low-cost sanitation, the people in rural areas entrusted Sulabh to construct Community Complexes on pay and use system.

Sulabh's entry in Rural Sanitation is only in later part of 1994-95. It has already installed nine community complexes in rural areas of five districts viz., Udaipur (2), Chittorgarh (1), Jaisalmer (2), Sawaimadhopur (3), and Dungarpur (1). The total cost of these Community Complexes amounts to Rs. 54.97 lakhs (the cost of which varies between Rs. 3.57 lakhs and 8.92 lakhs) according to the number of seats for toilets and bathing facilities provided for men and women. These complexes have been constructed at important location such as temples, bus stands and in four villages where large number of commuters visit every day.

Conclusion

Sulabh's achievement in implementation of household latrines and community complexes has been acknowledged by the people and State governments in urban areas. Sulabh's entry in rural areas by installation of community complexes has been appreciated by the people who are using its services and facilities. It may have a spread effect in other districts of Rajasthan.

13. GOA

Rural Sanitation Programme

The State of Goa, constituted on August 15, 1987, covers a total area of 3,702 sq. km. with a length of 105 km. from north to south and 60 km. width. It is situated on the slopes of Western Ghats, on borders of Karnataka and Maharashtra. As per 1991 Census, the total population of 11.70 lakhs comprises of 6.90 lakhs rural (59%) and 4.80 lakhs (41%) urban. Of the total population males 5.95 lakhs (50.85%) and females 5.75 lakhs (49.15%) are having literacy rates of 83.64 per cent and 67.09 per cent respectively. These literacy rates are far above when compared to All-India literacy rates.

Goa is divided into two districts North Goa and South Goa with their respective headquarters at Panaji and Margao. These two districts comprises of 11 talukas, 6 in North Goa and 5 in South Goa. There are 383 villages, out of which 360 villages are inhabited and the rest are uninhabited. There are 31 towns categorised as 13 census and 18 municipal towns. In rural areas, 1.36 lakhs households exist of which 1.30 households have to be provided Pour-Flush Water Seal (P.F.W.S) latrines.

Rural Sanitation Programme: SISSO's Initiative

The Public Health Engineering Divisions (PHED) of the Public

Works Department (PWD) is the nodal agency for rural sanitation programme. As the construction of PFWS latrines involved additional work, such as selection of site, awareness-building and motivation amongst beneficiaries for adoption of low-cost sanitation programme, the P.W.D invited Sulabh International Social Service Organisation (SISSO), a reputed Non-Governmental Organisation to perform these basic works. This was intended to ensure individual rural beneficiary participation in the programme. It is reported that through SISSO's initiative 19,807 units of PFWS latrines were constructed upto May 1998. In addition, 23,505 rural households were already having individual sanitary latrine facilities of different types.

The Government of Goa, therefore, prepared ten years Plan of Action (POA) to construct another 1,14,988 units of P.F.W.S. latrines in rural areas between 1995 and 2005. The estimated total project cost has been worked out as Rs. 83.26 crores. The unit cost of each latrine works out to Rs. 10,342 only along with superstructure, excluding the cost of land to be made available by beneficiary. Technical design and specifications are based as per Technical Advisory Group–T.A.G. Model No.81/014 under U.N.D.P.–India project, according to which Sulabh (SISSO) constructed 6,347 latrines. All these units are in use, affordable and acceptable to the rural community.

In order to achieve the target of 1,14,988 units of latrines, an yearly P.O.A. has been chalked out. It envisages construction of 9,929 units of latrines every year. This will benefit 51,593 persons every year. It is reported that between 1995 and 2005, 99,290 units of latrines will need to be constructed to reach the target. It is estimated that during this period of 10 years, about 5.16 lakhs persons will be benefited, by the low-cost sanitation programme, out of total rural population of 6.90 lakhs.

For meeting the total project cost of Rs. 83.26 crores, the Government of Goa has already allocated Rs. 20.81 crores (25%). The rest amount of Rs. 62.45 crores (75%) is proposed to be obtained through external financial assistance institutions. The P.O.A is to construct latrines for different income/target groups through own contrioutions and loan component (to be made available by the State government) as shown in the Table 2.21.

TABLE 2.21

Contribution and Loan Component

Income Group	Estimated PFWS Latrine Construction (Number)	Beneficiary Contribution (%)	Funds/Loans State Government (%)
Below Poverty Level (BPL)	33,442	Nil	100
Low Income Group (LIG)	41,215	25	75
Middle Income Group (MIG)	24,630	50	50

The Sulabh (SISSO) has been entrusted with the task of implementing the programme, which is being monitored by the P.H.E division.

Water Supply Programme

It is reported by the Directorate of Health Services, Goa that 41,211 persons (out-patients and in-patients) were treated for various water-borne diseases such as gastroenteritis, diarrhoea, viral hepatitis and typhoid fever during 1993. Out of total number of cases, large number 27,045 persons suffered from diarrhoea and 13,641 persons suffered from gastroenteritis. As many as 450 persons suffered from viral hepatitis and 175 persons from typhoid fever. Only 66 persons died due to water-borne diseases. Most significantly, cholera was not detected anywhere.

In order to provide safe drinking water to the entire rural population, an extensive regional water supply programme viz., Assonora, Sanquelim and Canacona are under implementation. With these programmes as well as Madai and Opa water supply schemes and other existing schemes, it is estimated to provide 70 LPCD safe drinking water within the next four years i.e., by the end of 1999 to the population of the entire State.

Assessment

The Government of Goa prepared an ambitious project to provide sanitation facilities for the entire rural community in Goa. The entire project was entrusted by the State Government to Sulabh International for implementation. It was estimated that 66,000 latrines were necessary for the 100 per cent coverage of rural Goa. Over 5,000 pour flush water-seal latrines are being constructed now in Goa every year. Considering that Goa is a small State with about 12 lakhs population, the coverage of over 15,000 families so far is significant towards achieving the goal of 100 per cent coverage.

Another prominent activity has been the construction and maintenance of community public toilets popularly known as Sulabh Shauchalaya Complexes. By June, 1998, 47 such complexes of varying capacity had been completed and work in the case of 8 complexes was in progress.

Goa is a tourist paradise, and the Department of Tourism came out in a big way to provide toilet facilities at major tourist centres. To be attractive to the tourists, the complexes were made architecturally beautiful and facilities such as cloak room, cooled drinking water, bathrooms were introduced at these complexes. The concept of the toilet being a dirty and stinking place is being successfully changed by Sulabh International in Goa. The complexes constructed after 1992 are better architecturally and are amenable to being maintained clean. The standard of specifications and of construction has been quite high. Another attractive feature of the toilet complexes has been the development and maintenance of small garden around them. This has made the toilet complexes look beautiful and attractive. The cleanliness and maintenance has been of a high order and the toilets are being used by the sophisticated citizens without any reservation. By the end of August 1998, Sulabh International Goa has been maintaining 48 community toilet complexes in Goa.

The most important aspect of the Sulabh International in Goa has been its ability to establish rapport and understanding with the authorities and the people. Its high credibility has been well acknowledged for its reliability.

Conclusion

When the Plan of Action 1995-2005 for rural sanitation and water supply programmes is implemented fully and if targets are realised fully, Goa will have the distinction of solving rural sanitation and water supply problems.

F. M. S. SWAMINATHAN RESEARCH FOUNDATION PROGRAMME

14. PONDICHERRY

Bio-Village Model

The Bio-village Model, developed by M.S. Swaminathan Research Foundation (MSSRF) and the Centre for Research on Sustainable Agriculture and Rural Development (CRSARD), Madras is a holistic approach based on an optimum utilization of existing physical and human resources for rural development. It attempts to integrate the principles of traditional systems with biological technologies to attain ecological sustainability by full utilization of agricultural and its allied production potential so that economic profitability may reach, particularly to the rural poor and women.

The Model also envisages to strengthen environmental sanitation and health care facilities with nutritional security to upgrade the standard and quality of life of the rural poor and women by introducing various programmes acceptable to the target group.

Evolution of Bio-Village Project

Since its inception in April 1990, the MSSRF developed the Bio-village concept to identify institutional capabilities for empowerment mechanism to achieve socio-economic growth and development. An intensive scientific feasibility study was conducted through eco-agro and socio-economic baseline survey to understand and assess various parameters of the current status of resources, institutions, infrastructure, potentials and constraints to promote human development through an integrated approach, farm and non-farm fruitful employment-generation activities for improving the standard and quality of life of the target groups, viz. women, educated/uneducated jobless youths, landless, marginal and small scale farmers.

Thus the Bio-village Project was initiated in 1991 with prioritisation of problem areas and participatory analysis techniques to gain confidence of the village people. The implementation of the Bio-village Project was started in three villages, viz., Pillayarkuppam, Sivaranthakam and Kizhur of Villnamur Commune Panchayat of the Union Territory of Pondicherry.

1. *Pillayarkuppam Bio-village*

The total land area of the village is 238.3 hectares, with a total population of 1829 (937 males and 892 females) as per 1991 Census. It is reported that 48 per cent of the people are illiterate, in which male and female illiteracy accounts for 36 per cent and 64 per cent respectively. There are 357 households constituting 147 landed and 210 landless households. The landless labourers and small farmers own land (between 0.5 and 1.0 ha) and marginal farmers (less than 0.5 ha). Because of the dry upland with sandy loam to sandy clay loam and a deep seated groundwater source (150-180 m), village resources are poor.

2. *Sivaranthakam Bio-village*

The total land area of the village is 176.3 hectares having a total population of 1204 (612 males and 592 females) as per 1991 Census. The illiteracy rate of this village has been recorded as 50 per cent in which the male and female illiteracy are of 41 per cent and 59 per cent respectively. Among the 233 households, 62 households comprise prosperous farmers with large holdings and they are co-habited with 171 landless households. The village is endowed with rich natural resources and agricultural potential as ground water source is at 60-100 m level.

3. *Kizhur Bio-village*

The total land area of the village is 135.1 hectares, having a total population of 857 (451 males and 406 females) as per 1991

Census. There are 48 per cent illiterates in the village, comprising of 45 per cent males and 55 per cent females. There are 163 households in the village composed of 65 landed households i.e., small-scale and medium scale farmers (owning between 1 and 2 ha) and 98 landless households. Dairy farming is the traditional occupation of the village.

It is significant to mention that the Bio-village Project in three villages viz., Pillayarkuppam, Sivaranthakam and Kizhur covers a total land area of about 550 ha and has a total population 3,890 in 753 households constituting 274 landed and 479 landless households. The Table 2.22 gives the details.

TABLE 2.22

Landed and Landless Households

Bio-villages	Total population	Landed household	Landless household	Total households
Pillayarkuppam	1829	147 (41%)	210 (59%)	357 (100%)
Sivaranthakam	1204	62 (26%)	171 (74%)	233 (100%)
Kizhur	857	65 (40%)	98 (60%)	163 (100%)
Total	3890	274 (36%)	479 (64%)	753 (100%)

Keeping in view the on-going government programme and value-added technological options for providing skilled jobs to the rural poor, women and youth in income-generating activities, the Bio-village Project envisages to educate and train rural youth/women in wood carving, terracotta, embroidery, making palm leaf articles, clay toys, doll making, fine crafts etc.

The Bio-village Model envisages also to improve the quality of human life within the capacity of supporting ecosystem with new materials, management strategies and marketing avenues based on decentralised production and centralised services to be provided to the community.

Some of the special features in Bio-village Model relevant to the present study of Environmental Sanitation and Health Aspects for Rural Development in Panchayati Raj are noted below:

(a) *Participatory Dialogue*

A major thrust of the Bio-village Model is the informal participatory dialogue between the Bio-village Consortium Coordination Committee, the bio-village scientists and the people such as farmers, landless labourers, women and youth as well as concerned government officials in order to prioritise the needs of food production; to create awareness of employment-generation potentials and constraints in rural development as well as to identify appropriate technological options suitable to socio-economic and ecological conditions; to assess the techno-infrastructural needs for promoting marketing; and above all to gain confidence of the people by implementing the: (i) on-farm research and development programmes, and (ii) off-farm research and development programmes.

With the process of participatory dialogue twelve enterprises were identified in 1991-92 and four of them were tested for adoption. The identified enterprises, interventions and primary beneficiaries are stated in Table 2.23.

TABLE 2.23

Households Participating in Selected Enterprises

Enterprises		Households
1.	Goat Rearing	Landless women
2.	Group Sericulture	-do-
3.	Fodder Bank	-do-
4.	Hybrid Vegetable Seeds	-do-
5.	Mushroom Production	-do-
6.	Jasmine Cultivation	Marginal Farm Women
7.	Family Nutrition Security	Landless women, Marginal Farm Women, Small Farmer
8.	Broiler Production	Landless women, Marginal Farm Women
9.	Composite Pisciculture	Landless poor people
10.	Environmental Sanitation	-do-
11.	Azolla Bio-fertilizer Farmer	Marginal Farmer, Small Farmer
12.	Recycling of Biowastes	-do-

(b) Environmental Sanitation and Health Measures

(i) One of the features of the Bio-village Project is to create awareness about the importance of environmental sanitation for a healthy living. In this regard, the project got installed five Pour-Flush Twin-Pit toilets in five households of landless poor people in Pillayarkuppam village. These toilets were installed by the Sulabh International Social Service Organisation, as a demonstration for its effective use by the beneficiaries during 1992-93. It has indeed created an impact amongst the target group who want to get this facility installed in their household not only in this village but also in Sivanthankam and Kizhur Bio-villages. There is an urge among the local community to get public toilets atleast in schools of these villages. But Community Complex toilets and bio-gas plants based on human excreta and/or solid waste for environmental upgradation are still to be tackled for lack of community cohesiveness and social inhibitions.

After field visits to all the three Bio-villages, it is observed that much headway has still to be made in regard to safe drinking water supply and removal of stagnation of waste water around public stand post, in drains, roads, and bylanes and even in the neighbourhood of many households. The problem areas of environmental sanitation causing health hazards in Bio-villages have still to be identified. Effective awareness campaign and advocacy for environmental sanitation and health measures have to be taken not only at the level of households of rural poor but also in the whole Bio-village by promoting sanitary latrines/ facilities as a package.

(ii) *Nutrition Garden*: As an aspect of health measure the Project initiated Nutrition Garden in village school of Pillayarkuppam where vegetables are produced for midday meal programme. Besides, pomegranate and acid lime fruit trees have been planted with bamboo fencing. School staff and children were trained to grow and maintain these vegetables and fruits. The project established household Nutrition Gardens to improve the health status in the backyards of 12 households in Sivaranthakam, 5 households in Pillayarkuppam and 5 in Kizhur. The inmates of these households were trained to grow and maintain vegetables such as okra, brinjal, chilli, tomato, amaranths and radish as well as fruits namely, lime, pomegranate, as also curry leaves etc.

The vegetables production and marketing management have had a salutary impact not only on the health status of the target group but also raised the per-capita monthly income of landless labour women/rural poor from the level of Rs. 300 per month to over Rs. 1000 per month which is the most encouraging feature as a job-led economic growth strategy of the Bio-village Project.

(c) The Bio-village Project, after gaining experience through many initiatives of techno-infrastructural development and income/employment-generating activities have formulated a "Bio-village Pilot Demonstration Project" covering thirteen villages of the Villianur Community Panchayat in 1993-94 and submitted it to the United Nations Development Programmes (UNDP) for support. The areas of technology intervention on the farm research and development including environmental sanitation and skilled technological empowerment for income and employment-generation activities have now been identified. Besides, the Project has endeavoured to tap all possible support from the government agencies concerned with rural development. For example, the supply of safe drinking water and street lighting in Pillayankuppam village for the rural poor in M.E.R colony, has been ensured by formation of a 13-member maintenance committee. Further, Bio-village Consortium has been constituted in June 1993 for the implementation of different programmes conceived in the Project.

Assessment

The Biovillage project of sustainable agriculture and rural development was launched in three villages viz. Pillayarkuppam, Sivaranthakam and Kizhur of Villnamur Commune Panchayat of the Union Territory of Pondicherry as a demonstration project in April 1990. The support of the UNDP was extended to test and demonstrate the Biovillage paradigm in 19 villages spread over in about 3,700 hectares with a population of about 25,000 in January 1995.

The Biovillage Model has developed a new paradigm of

rural development to address the main problems of resource degradation and rural poverty. It recognises group action as the key strategy to deliver and sustain development initiatives. Some of the activities of Biovillage paradigm as adopted in technologies and intervention under specific biophysical and socio-economic conditions, and technological empowerment of the resource poor by translating technologies into income generation activities for resource poor, were terminated by March 1996 as reported in the Annual Report of 1995-96.

The Report states that the focus on alleviation of rural poverty were developed under four general categories:

1. Identification of environmental friendly, economically viable, socially acceptable technologies and interventions through participatory on-farm research and development. This took up the concerned areas such as Hybrid rice seed production, and its testing and demonstration; Evaluation of the suitability of biofertilisers and green manures; and Integrated Crop Management trials, were, for example, the specific target areas.
2. Secondly, enterprises for enhancing livelihood security was concerned with mushroom production by rural women; group sericulture; goat rearing and fodder shrub based biofences; dairying for the resource poor; vegetable production for marginal and small farmers; jasmine cultivation and homestead nutrition garden. All these activities were done by translating technology into production and employment generation activities.
3. Lastly, cost-effective support services was extended as a method of group organisation and management at different centres in three demonstration biovillages in vermiculture, biocentre institutions and marketing particularly vegetables, mushroom vermicompost, floriculture, sericulture. For all these activities market database as production of agricultural produce and its marketing in regulated market was documented.

This Biovillage Project Model had all along been working closely with the concerned Government departments under the guidance of Development Commissioner, Pondicherry and the

The Indian Bank, as a lead bank, for the project as well as research scientists and field officers of the MSS Research Foundation.

With regard to Environmental Sanitation, 5 single household toilets constructed by Sulabh International created demand for more household toilets, which led to construction of 15 more toilets in Pillayarkuppam, 5 toilets in Kizhur and 8 toilets in Sivaranthakam. It is really encouraging to note that 30% of the cost of construction of toilets was met by the resident of each household. This is being promoted in other 16 villages of the project area.

Besides individual household toilets, the project is encouraging to construct soak-pits in order to avoid water logging around the houses being released through Kitchen and bath cubicles. Many masons have been trained to construct two-pit pour flush household toilets as an environmental sanitation drive in the project area.

The Biovillage Project Model is in progress in the Union Territory of Pondicherry with the support of UNDP. It is heartening to note that the programme has been placed for long-term approaches by integrating its work with the core activities of J.R.D. Tata Ecotechnology Centre and significant activities undertaken by the B.V. Rao Centre for Sustainable Food Security. Both these centres have extended financial support to MSS Research Foundation to promote integrated rural development.

Conclusion

It may be concluded, as a general observation that the Biovillage Project covering three villages of the Union Territory of Pondicherry has demonstrated that the 'entry point' even for the rural poor and women could be 'sustainable agriculture' which is the backbone of the rural community. The objectives could be achieved by proper identification of enterprises through market-driven approach, appropriate technology, training, techno-infrastructure and trade. In this process of rural development, including environment-friendly social and economic activities for income and employment-generation, the role of information, education and communication is of vital importance. It is only then the fruits of development may reach those who need it the most.

G. SRI SATHYA SAI WATER SUPPLY PROJECT

15. ANANTHPUR DISTRICT – ANDHRA PRADESH

Introduction

Sri Sathya Sai Water Supply Project initiated by Sri Sathya Sai Baba of Prasanthi Nilayam in Ananthpur district of Andhra Pradesh is an exclusive Water Supply Project (WSP) Model in India. This model is an expression of vision of unfathomable and expansive love of Sri Sathya Sai Baba to provide one of the basic and vital resources of Nature to Humanity. It is through this project sponsored by Sri Sathya Sai (SSS) Central Trust by investing Rs. 300 crores, millions of men and animals (who lived for generations in drought and despair) in more than 700 villages in Ananthpur district have been now provided safe drinking water to their 'parched lips'.

Demography: Ananthpur District

The total population of Andhra Pradesh was 6.65 crores with an area covering 2,75,045 sq. kms having 23 districts in 1991 census. The rural and urban population were 4.86 crores and 1.79 crores respectively, having total number of households in rural areas 1.03 crores and 0.37 crores in urban areas respectively in 1991 census.

Among 23 districts, Ananthpur district was having a total population of 3.18 lakhs constituting an area of 19,130 sq. kms in 1991 census. The rural and urban population were recorded as 2.43 lakhs and 0.75 lakh respectively. In Ananthpur district there were 12 urban centres having more than thousand villages.

Prasanthi Nilayam is one of the urban centres and has been now declared as township among 12 urban centres of the district. The total population of Prasanthi Nilayam was 1,005 only in 1991 census but presently it is estimated that the total population may be over 2000. It is also estimated that every day the floating population from various parts of India and abroad may be about

TABLE 2.24
Proportion (Percentage) of Electricity, Safe Drinking Water and Toilet Facilities

Name of State/ District/Urban Agglomeration City/ Town	Total Rural Urban	Population	Elect-ricity	Safe drink-ing water	Toilet	Electri-city and drinking water	Toilet and safe drinking water	Electri-city and toilet	All the three facili-ties	None of the three facilities
ANDHRA PRADESH										
Anantapur District	Total	3,181,814	54.04	84.86	10.81	45.63	9.43	9.99	8.75	6.59
	Rural	2,435,761	49.25	83.29	3.72	40.43	3.05	2.92	2.40	7.74
	Urban	748,053	70.90	90.38	35.81	63.96	31.94	34.91	31.14	2.57
Urban Agglomeration										
Anantapur (M)	Urban	174,924	78.66	92.36	49.80	72.66	45.13	48.99	44.37	1.60
Guntakal (M)	Urban	107,592	65.23	88.87	33.92	58.27	30.82	33.48	30.53	4.01
Hindupur (M)	Urban	104,651	68.92	95.45	36.96	65.31	34.66	35.87	33.62	0.88
Dharmavaram (M)	Urban	78,961	72.93	90.31	26.53	66.59	23.75	25.43	22.64	3.35
Gooty (P)	Urban	37,814	78.12	75.59	31.83	59.30	26.17	31.45	25.86	5.51
Kadiri (M)	Urban	63,378	67.29	81.95	38.64	53.72	29.32	36.55	27.57	4.14
Kalyandurg (P)	Urban	23,106	67.48	94.30	27.67	64.44	26.82	26.82	25.97	2.67
Penukonda (P)	Urban	17,030	78.90	95.91	38.74	75.75	36.38	37.64	35.43	0.79
Prasanthi - Nilayam (TS)	Urban	1,005	100.00	93.83	100.00	93.83	93.83	100.00	93.83	0.00
Rayadurg (M)	Urban	40,845	59.54	94.51	22.79	56.57	20.86	21.90	20.12	2.38
Tadpatri (M)	Urban	71,068	66.43	93.60	27.32	61.72	24.65	26.72	24.09	1.66
Uravakonda (P)	Urban	27,679	68.04	83.67	17.84	55.24	13.21	17.44	12.90	3.43

Source: Registrar General and Census Commissioner, India; Census of India 1991, Housing and Amenities - Occasional Paper No. 5 of 1994, pp. 76.

10,000 to 12,000 persons, who come to visit this pilgrimage township for the last several decades. This population has also to be served with basic services everyday such as electricity, safe drinking water and toilet facilities. The Census of India 1991 recorded the provision of such facilities, particularly in 12 urban centres of the district as shown in Table 2.24.

Collaborators

It was the spirit of Sri Sathya Sai Baba which widened the scope of awareness amongst three collaborators, in this Water Supply Mission, viz., the SSS Central Trust, Government of Andhra Pradesh and the implementing agency Larsen and Tubro Limited (ECC Construction Group) leader in the field of construction expertise and project management.

Implementation

Actually, Sri Sathya Sai Baba's vision was evident in November 1994. But the project was conceived in March - April 1995 and formulated by August 1995. Then the three collaborators and actors discussed the implementation strategy and completed the project in about 15 months, i.e., by December 1996 and the project was commissioned in March-April 1997. In other words, the whole water supply project was conceived, formulated, implemented and commissioned in a record time. It has been a monumental achievement of the Water Supply Project, so far not heard, but seen in this part of the world, where gentle laughter ripples in about 731 villages and three urban centres such as Ananthpur (Municipality), Kadiri (Municipality) and Prasanthi Nilayam (Township) out of 12 urban centres in Ananthpur district of Andhra Pradesh.

Schemes of the Project

Sri Sathya Sai Water Supply Project consists of four schemes:

(i) *Comprehensive Protected Water Supply Scheme*: This involves infiltration wells, collection wells and associated pumping behind the Chitravati Balancing Reservoir at

Peddakotla and Chinnakotla villages covering 169 villages. Sources for other infiltration wells includes Pennar and Hagari rivers, which covers 93 villages.

(ii) Direct pumping from Pennar Ahobilam Balancing Reservoir (PABR) and treatment through rapid sand filtration system. This consists of two major lines passing through Kalyandurg and Atmakur covering 93 villages.

(iii) Comprehension Water Supply Scheme (CWSS) through seven summer storage tanks ranging upto 100 acres by tapping water from Tungabhadra High Level Canal (when water flows in canal) covering 97 villages.

(iv) The Protected Water Supply Scheme (PWS) covering 279 villages. It involves drilling deep bore wells, construction of storage tanks and installation of pipeline networks.

Salient Features of the Project

Sri Sathya Sai Water Supply Project consists of six salient features:

(i) Laying of more than 2000 km of AC, C1 and D1, MS and PVC pipelines and their diameter ranges from 80 mm to 600 mm. These parts were transported in thousands of trucks and dozen of railway wagons from different parts of the country in course of about 70 to 90 days.

(ii) Installation of 43 pumps from 1 lakh litre capacity to 25 lakh litres capacity.

(iii) Construction of 18 Balancing Reservoirs at the top of hillocks with capacities ranging from 3 lakh litres to 10 lakh litres.

(iv) Construction of 270 overhead reservoirs, Capacity ranging from 40,000 litres to 3,00,000 litres.

(v) 125 Ground Level Reservoir. Capacity ranging from 20,000 litres to 80,000 litres.

(vi) Installation of more than 1500 per cent concrete cisterns of 2,500 litres capacity with provision of four taps to be used by villagers.

Conclusion

The Draft Ninth Five Year Plan document suggest replication of Sri Sathya Sai Water Supply (WSP) Project Model. Our comments are:

(i) Initiation, formulation and implementation of this type of Project Model, as achieved in Prasanthi Nilayam of Ananthpur district, with massive investment only by Sri Sathya Sai Central Trust amounting to Rs. 300 crores within a period of less than 15 months is not possible to replicate any where in the country. It not only needs resources but also vision and will-power, dedication and commitment by each implementing agency, concerned people and beneficiary in the project. It is a rare and exclusive example.

(ii) Secondly, the whole project was handed over to the State Government of Andhra Pradesh district administration and local bodies of the urban and rural bodies for maintenance of all the four schemes stated in this report. It is reported that several anomalies and hindrances have since occurred which needs attention. It is too early to make any valid assessment of the project. While the effort is laudable, its sustainability has to be still verified.

CHAPTER - III

SANITATION, HEALTH AND PANCHAYATI RAJ: A MODEL

OUR search for a model has ended. We have in previous pages narrated in great detail the essential features of each and every model in heterogeneous population. During the course of our narration it has also been brought out emphatically that the primary health care strategy, among others, considers safe water and appropriate sanitation as a cornerstone of basic Health For All (HFA).

The broad contours of a model have been spelt out both in the Eighth Five-Year Plan (1992-97) document as also the General Guidelines for Implementation of Centrally Sponsored Rural Sanitation Programme. Under the title "Thrust and Strategies" the Plan document* declares that, "the concept of total sanitation – covering primary health care, water availability, women's welfare, immunisation and provision of sanitation facilities, all linked to cleanliness as a basic human need – will be emphasised . . . it is suggested that the Rural Sanitation Programme be restructured providing for the following elements:

(a) all activities under this programme will be undertaken through local body/village Panchayat and with beneficiary participation;

* Eighth Five-Year Plan document, Vol II, p. 381.

(b) wherever feasible, NGOs will be involved in the implementation of the programme;

(c) women will be actively associated with the implementation of the programme;

(d) some contribution should be solicited from the beneficiaries, at least in the form of physical labour, in order to engender among them the realisation that the assets created belong to the local community.

The general guidelines for implementation of Centrally Sponsored Rural Sanitation Programmes, *inter alia* prescribes that each State should develop at least one Model Village every year under the Integrated Rural Sanitation Programme covering facilities like, sanitary latrines, conversion of dry latrines, garbage pits, soak-pits, drains, pavement of lanes; sanitary latrines in *anganwadis*, schools, panchayat ghar, health centre; smokeless chulahs; cleanliness of ponds and tanks; clean surroundings around stand posts, handpumps, wells and other drinking water sources with platform including washing and bathing platforms etc.

While we are not in a position to certify or authenticate the exact number of Model Villages so far developed in each State, what we are certain about is that the intention of the policy-makers is to develop prototype models, which are not only replicable but also sustainable and have three essential elements:

(1) the concept of total sanitation.

(2) involvement of both panchayats and Non-Governmental Organisations (NGOs); and

(3) beneficiary contribution in one form or other in lesser or greater volume.

During our field visits throughout the length and breadth of our country, we saw different agencies vying with each other for attaining the goal of total rural sanitation, of course with different methodologies to develop 'Model Villages'. In some cases, one or the other prominent features spelt out by Planning Commission or Ministry of Rural Development (now Ministry of Rural Areas and Employment) figured prominently. We shall discuss the situation case by case to delineate the characteristics of each model qualifying for being replicated, of course with essential alterations to suit local requirements in every single area.

It is pertinent to emphasise that the "Concept of Total Sanitation" has meaning and content only when it is people-friendly, ecologically suited as well as affordable and acceptable to each and every situation, which alter even within a development block or a multi-ethnic large habitation.

A close study of the stipulations of the Planning Commission and the guidelines of the Ministry of Rural Development would reveal that the following features in lesser or more degree must be present in Model Villages under Rural Sanitation Programme:

1. Activities to be undertaken through local body/village panchayats.
2. Beneficiary participation
3. Involvement of NGOs
4. Women to be actively associated
5. Facilities should not be on 100 per cent subsidy basis, some contribution from beneficiary atleast in the shape of physical labour must be insisted.
6. Integrated rural sanitation programme must consist of sanitary latrine at household and institutional levels (schools, panchayat ghar etc.)
7. Health coverage
8. Smokeless Chulhas
9. Environmental Sanitation
10. Safe-drinking water

Let us now recapitulate the ingredients of different models in different States described in Chapter II, under UNICEF, World Bank, Sulabh and M.S.S. Research Foundation assisted programmes. This will enable us to clarify whether they qualify for being considered as a Model under Government of India prescription, though in fact, they may be rendering yeoman's service on many counts; promoting environmental sanitation and health status in rural areas. In any case a distinction will need to be made between a project model and a model village. A model village could also adopt different project models to provide specific services.

First, the Periyar Model in Tamil Nadu. It has health, education and sanitation components to the desired extent with people's involvement especially women in large numbers. The Periyar project also provides an excellent illustration that the integrated rural sanitation programme can be implemented through government functionaries and infrastructure with active support of Panchayati Raj Institutions and to a limited extent, NGO support. It would be unfair to discard the merits of the project on grounds that it is not wholly implemented through panchayat. In any case, this is one model which could at least be a flag-bearer for governmental initiative in successfully executing a rural sanitation programme in a unified and composite manner. The Periyar Model has its merits, though under the decentralised administration it would be preferable to implement it through panchayats.

The Midnapore Model which is being implemented by the Lokshiksha Parishad, Ramakrishna Mission, in Midnapore district, West Bengal is based on locally available low-cost technology, and materials to suit various income groups with unit cost ranging from Rs. 230 to Rs. 3,030 only. An important feature of the Midnapore Model is that it is based on the concept of Self-Reliance, without any Government subsidy (except SCs/STs) by articulating the needs of the people through local Youth Clubs, Mahila Mandals, Panchayati Raj Institutions and other local institutions. The development of the concept of "Self-Financing Scheme and Social Marketing" approach is an enviable achievement, which has potential of being replicated elsewhere as a sustainable programme.

UNICEF participation in developing community based approaches to rural sanitation so as to be in consonance with socio-economic diversity of our population has been commendable. The Alwar Model (Rajasthan) began in 1987 aimed at motivating community to adopt a package of sanitary facilities and practices through a cadre of sanitation motivators at village level with the State Rural Development and Panchayati Raj Department playing a catalytic nodal agency role. The fact that the State government contemplates to implement more or less the same model in all the thirty districts of the State (UNICEF collaborating in 17 districts only) is an indication of the acceptance of the model by the people. The State government has also introduced some innovative changes in the project to be more effective. Proposal to establish Rural Sanitary Mart, construct Facility Park for women, imparting training to various categories of people and to enlist assistance of NGOs are steps in right direction. Perhaps, involvement of panchayats would be the next needed step. The fact that Alwar Model has created a spread effect is testimony of the efficacy of the package.

Tha Allahabad Model (Uttar Pradesh) started with UNICEF support in 1989-90, indeed influenced the State government's policy on sanitation. The project has a three-pronged approach to promote rural sanitation and particularly in regard to sanitation coverage through household latrines. The first one is with a subsidy of Rs. 1200 and with Rs. 300 from the beneficiary; the second with Rs. 450 as subsidy and the rest from the beneficiary; and the third with no subsidy, the beneficiary is provided with only technical guidance and facilities for creating the necessary infrastructure. The Institute of Engineering and Rural Technology (IERT) is implementing this model. Although our findings do not lend support to compliment the execution of the Model, yet it must be admitted that the Model has three prominent characteristics:

1. The low-cost materials for construction of household latrines and sanitary facilities using locally available resources;
2. The scheme of training of Master Masons in the IERT; and
3. The effect to eliminate subsidy component might succeed, which will then be one of the components of the model village being attained.

The policy of the State Department of Panchayati Raj for promotion of Rural Sanitation Programme along with panchayat udyogs at different locations is in process in 63 districts of Uttar Pradesh (out of which UNICEF is collaborating in 13 districts after adopting some of the features of Allahabad Model). One of the findings, however, reveals that the "community participation in the entire process has been limited" and speaks about the lack of effectiveness of the programme as a whole in Uttar Pradesh.

The World Bank assists programmes of Rural Water Supply and Sanitation. In our report (chapter II) we have described World Bank assisted programmes of Rural Sanitation in Gujarat as well as other programmes being implemented in Gujarat to promote sanitation in the whole State. We have also described Rural Water Supply and Sanitation Programmes in Karnataka and Maharashtra with a physical and financial time target utilising World Bank assistance. These specific programmes may not exactly qualify for being considered as a model, yet we dealt with these projects in our report to provide a global account of sanitary schemes prevailing in our country and to appreciate in its proper perspective the significance of each model.

The Sulabh International Social Service Organisation (SISSO) Model, a synonym to low-cost sanitation in our country, revolves around motivation, promotion, education and community participation. The contribution of SISSO in urban sanitation, especially the 'pay and use' community complex concept, are too well known in our country and abroad. SISSO have developed many designs for latrines based on the use of low-cost based materials. An appropriate delivery system ensures adequate software support and community participation.

We have in this report discussed only a small part of their activities restricted to the concept of "Model Village". These are in the States of Haryana, Orissa, Bihar, Rajasthan and Goa. The cornerstone of their edifice of "Model Village" is people, services and facilities, following the dictates of people. When the Teekli Model village in Sohna Block of Gurgaon district in Haryana is fully developed, it will stand out as an exquisite example of well thought out formulations and ably executed schemes with people's involvement spearheaded by the village panchayat in bringing out perceptible changes in their march towards a better living. The Teekli Village Model has all the ingredients spelt out by official quarters. We are unable, however, to pronounce a definite opinion about the success of the project because it is premature to do so, for it was launched only in July 1994.

Orissa district model developed by SISSO with active financial support from the State government seeks to answer rural sanitation problems at the macro level with focus on villages. The two coastal districts of Puri and Ganjam have their own ecological and environmental constraints. Evolving suitable techniques to answer each individual situation is the endeavour of SISSO.

Sulabh is no stranger to Bihar, for the organisation was founded and nurtured by a committed person, belonging to Bihar. Their entry in the field of rural sanitation and their programmes in Samastipur and Gaya to develop district models, similar to that in Orissa, is an attempt to introduce new strategies to tackle adequately the problems for rural sanitation.

M. S. Swaminathan Research Foundation, Madras is a recent entrant in the field of sanitation though their contribution towards sustainable agriculture, environmental promotion and biological technologies have been of a longer duration. Evolution of three bio-villages in Pondicherry is a creditable approach. The contributions of Sulabh in providing low-cost sanitary latrines is noteworthy. The experiment has demonstrated that the "entry point" for rural sanitation could as well be sustainable agriculture. This lends a new dimension to our approach. Perhaps, in future projects this and such relevant "entry points" might emerge and that would herald a new era for healthy living with multiple options amongst our deserving rural population.

The Alma-Ata Declaration of 1978 identified Primary Health Care as crucial to the attainment of World Health Organisation's (WHO) call of Health For All (HFA) by 2000 A.D. This included provision for safe-drinking water and adequate sanitation as one of the essential components to bring about improvement in health. WHO is the main U.N. agency collaborating with India in developing health care capabilities including water supply and sanitation. Generally, WHO provides assistance on a biennium basis through the following services:

1. Supplies and Equipments
2. Training/Fellowships/Study Tours
3. Short-term Consultancy

4. Subsidy for Group Educational Activities/Seminars/ Workshops/Conferences/Studies etc.

At this stage it would be appropriate to have futuristic imperatives in evolving an alternative model with regard to the scope and possibilities of a healthy sanitation regime, under the newly enacted Panchayati Raj provisions.

In his book *Panchayati Raj in India: From Legislation to Movement*, George Mathew notes that the story of Panchayati Raj in India was well brought out by the Asoka Mehta Committee in 1978 when it identified three phases in the life of Panchayati Raj, starting from inception till 1977; (a) the phase of ascendancy, 1959 to 1964, (b) the phase of stagnation, 1965 to 1969, and (c) the phase of decline, 1969 to 1977. In fact, the decline after 1977 was more rapid. The sanitation and health aspects in rural areas received treatment in consonance with the health of the Panchayati Raj institutions themselves, notwithstanding the tremendous pace in expansion of community development and other related Plan programmes. It was unfortunate that rural sanitation and rural health measures did not receive the attention they deserved primarily due to the absence of an effective "people's front" like Panchayati Raj institutions. The hopes were kindled and aspirations were high with the enactment of the Constitution (Seventy-third Amendment) Act 1992 incorporating Part IX in the Constitution with regard to the panchayats. This was indeed the culmination of an eventful phase in the march towards realisation of a working democracy of the Indian Union guaranteeing decentralised functioning. While it is too early to assess with objectivity the results, because even the mandatory elections according to the stipulations have not been completed as yet in some States, it is in all probability evolving into an effective instrument for change in the pattern and implementation of rural area development programmes. This expectation is based mainly on pragmatic considerations arising out of schematic structure of Panchayati Raj, as incorporated in the 73rd Constitution Amendment Act, and as reflected in the individual State Panchayat Acts. The vital ingredient in the shaping of rural scene for the decent comfortable living is the envisaged items of activities suggested to be controlled by local government institutions listed out in the Eleventh Schedule to the Constitution. The complete Schedule is given below:

ELEVENTH SCHEDULE

(Article 243 G)

1. Agriculture, including agricultural extension.
2. Land improvement, implementation of land reforms, land consolidation and soil conservation.
3. Minor irrigation, water management and watershed development.
4. Animal husbandry, dairying and poultry.
5. Fisheries.
6. Social forestry and farm forestry.
7. Minor forest produce.
8. Small scale industries, including food processing industries.
9. Khadi, village and cottage industries.
10. Rural housing.
11. Drinking water.
12. Fuel and fodder
13. Roads, culverts, bridges, ferries, waterways and other means of communication.
14. Rural electrification, including distribution of electricity.
15. Non-conventional energy sources.
16. Poverty alleviation programme.
17. Education, including primary and secondary schools.
18. Technical training and vocational education
19. Adult and non-formal education.
20. Libraries.
21. Cultural activities.
22. Markets and fairs.
23. Health and sanitation, including hospitals, primary health centres and dispensaries.
24. Family Welfare.
25. Women and child development.
26. Social welfare, including welfare of the handicapped and mentally retarded.
27. Welfare of the weaker sections, and in particular, of the Scheduled Castes and Scheduled Tribes.

28. Public distribution system.
29. Maintenance of community assets.

A perusal of the Schedule would reveal that in so far as the subject matter of this report is concerned, the panchayats could tackle, given the requisite financial and administrative support, the problems of rural sanitation and health in view of items (10) rural housing, (11) drinking water, (16) poverty alleviation programme, (23) health and sanitation including hospitals, primary health centres and dispensaries, and (29) maintenance of community assets. In particular, Article, 243 G of the Constitution specifically enjoins that, "subject to the provisions of this Constitution, the Legislature of a State may, by law, endow the panchayats with such powers and authority as may be necessary to enable them to function as institutions of self-government and such law may contain provisions for the devolution of powers and responsibilities upon panchayats at the appropriate level, subject to such conditions as may be specified therein, with respect to –

(a) the preparation of plans for economic development and social justice;
(b) the implementation of schemes for economic development and social justice as may be entrusted to them including those in relation to the matters listed in the Eleventh Schedule.

Article 243-I of the Constitution provides for the setting up of a Finance Commission to review the financial position of the panchayats and to make recommendations to the Governor as to:

(1) (a) the principles which should govern–

(i) the distribution between the State and the Panchayats of the net proceeds of the taxes, duties, tolls and fees leviable by the State, which may be divided between them under this Part and the allocation between the Panchayats at all levels of their respective shares of such proceeds;

(ii) the determination of the taxes, duties, tolls and fees which may be assigned to, or appropriated by, the Panchayats;

(iii) the grants-in-aid to the Panchayats from the consolidated Fund of the State;

(b) the measures needed to improve the financial position of the Panchayats;

(c) any other matter referred to the Finance Commission by the Governor in the interests of sound finance of the Panchayats.

(2) The Legislature of a State may, by law, provide for the composition of the Commission, the qualifications of which shall be requisite for appointment as members thereof and the manner in which they shall be selected.

(3) The Commission shall determine their procedure and shall have such powers in the performance of their functions as the Legislature of the State may, by law, confer on them.

(4) The Governor shall cause every recommendation made by the Commission under this Article together with an explanatory memorandum as to the action taken thereon to be laid before the Legislature of the State.

As per information available as on 31 July, 1995, 17 States, namely, Andhra Pradesh, Assam, Bihar, Gujarat, Haryana, Himachal Pradesh, Karnataka, Kerala, Madhya Pradesh, Maharashtra, Manipur, Punjab, Rajasthan, Tamil Nadu, Tripura, Uttar Pradesh and West Bengal have constituted State Finance Commissions. It may be mentioned that the provision in the Constitution is applicable to 21 States. The States which have not constituted Finance Commissions during the reference period are Arunachal Pradesh, Goa, Orissa and Sikkim.

Panchayati Raj: The Concept and Practice - The Hiatus

Regular periodic elections to the Panchayati Raj institutions is one of the basic elements of the Constitutional amendment. It is unfortunate that in some cases, this primary requirement was not followed.

Election to the Panchayat Bodies in conformity with the Act was announced between 1993 and 1994 in 22 States viz., Andhra Pradesh, Arunachal Pradesh, Assam, Bihar, Goa, Gujarat, Haryana, Himachal Pradesh, Jammu and Kashmir. (Panchayat dissolved on February 24, 1997 by the Supreme Court and again Panchayati Raj Act was passed in 1989), Karnataka, Kerala, Madhya Pradesh, Maharashtra, Manipur, Orissa, Rajasthan, Sikkim, Tamil Nadu, Tripura, Uttar Pradesh and West Bengal. However, elections could not be held between 1994 and 1998 in all these States.

The peculiar cases of the six States i.e., Assam, Bihar, Karnataka, Kerala, Orissa and Tamil Nadu with regard to conducting elections as per the 73rd Constitutional Amendment Act are discussed below. The Act (under Article 243-B) specifies that "there shall be constituted in every State, Panchayat at the village, intermediate and district levels". It is, therefore, mandatory to hold elections to the Panchayats after their term is over or they are dissolved earlier. But in Assam, Bihar, Karnataka, Kerala, Orissa and Tamil Nadu elections were postponed for one reason or another.

Assam

The last Panchayat election was conducted in 1986. The Assam PR Act 1994 envisaged three-tier panchayat institutions. The then Chief Minister announced election to Zilla Parishads in March 1994 but it was postponed for October 1994. Subsequently, the State Election Commission announced that election would be delayed due to framing of election rules, delimitation of constituencies and preparation of electoral rolls and its printing etc. Meanwhile, the tenure of Panchayats expired in 1997. The State Assembly adopted a resolution to hold election in August 1997 or by the end of the year after the High Court intervened in the matter. But the election has not taken place till January 1999.

Bihar

The last Gram Panchayat elections were held in 1978. The new PR Act was enacted on August 23, 1993. The then Chief Minister promised to hold elections in August 1994, but it was postponed due to re-delimitation and lack of complete list of Backward classes (BC). In December 1995 in response to a public litigation petition, the High Court directed the State Government to hold elections at the earliest. The government proposed January 17, 19, 21 and 23, 1995 as dates for conducting the elections to Gram Panchayats, but it was not done. In order to protect the interests of the State Election Commission (SEC) for violating the High Court directives and contempt of court, the SEC filed a petition in the court that the State Government did not provide facilities for conducting elections. Hence, the High Court struck down several provisions of the Bihar Panchayat Act, including the reservation for the BCs. It ruled that total reservations in any elected body could not exceed 50 per cent of the total seats (although the Act had proposed 75 per cent reservation for Scheduled Castes, Scheduled Tribes and Backward classes). At last, the High Court directed the government to hold elections to the Gram Panchayats after completion of the Parliamentary polls, within six months, in 1996. Thereafter, the State Government appealed to the Supreme Court which is still pending. Thus, the elections to panchayats are still to be held.

Karnataka

The last elections to the Gram Panchayats were held on December 29, 1993 under the provision of the new Act. It was announced after several postponement that the elections would be held on April 27, 1994. The State Election Commission announced its further postponement on account of social tensions and assured to hold elections to Taluk and Zilla Parishads by December 1994. After hearing, the Supreme Court extended the time upto March 1995 for all the elections to take place, which was actually held on March 13 and 15, 1995.

Kerala

After the Panchayats were dissolved, the new Panchayati Raj Act was passed on April 23, 1994. The Scheduled elections during September 1994 was later postponed to April 1995 were not held. Finally elections were completed on September 23-25, 1995.

Orissa

Elections to the Gram Panchayats and Panchayat Samitis were held in May-June 1992 before the commencement of the 73rd Amendment Act. On account of non-availability of ballot boxes, the elections to Zilla Parishads were postponed on various occasions till November 1994. However, on August 1, 1995 the new government dissolved all the 5,623 Gram Panchayats, 314 Panchayat Samitis and 96 municipalities as these bodies did not provide for reservations for SCs/STs under the provisions of 73rd and 74th Constitution Amendment Acts. It was announced that elections to the local bodies would be held during January 1996, but it was postponed by the High Court till June-July 1996 after hearing public petition of political parties. The Supreme Court directed the State Government to hold elections to the local bodies and the SEC issued notification for holding elections between January 11 and 25, 1997. The State Government requested the Supreme Court to postpone elections on account of severe drought in some parts of the State. The State Election Commission objected on which the court did not give any ruling. Finally, the elections to Panchayats were held between January 11 and 25, 1997.

Tamil Nadu

Earlier elections to the Panchayats were held in 1970 and 1986. The new Panchayat Raj Act was enforced on April 24, 1994 and the local bodies were under special officers. Elections to the Panchayats and the local bodies were postponed on several excuses till December 1995 such as: delimitation of constituencies, earmarking of seats for reserved categories, revision of electoral rolls, tenure of the special officers etc. In

June 1995, the Governor addressed the State Assembly in which it was announced to reserve half the seats to Backward classes at all the three levels. In October 1995, the State Election Commission announced that elections to all the PRIs would be held between December 1 and 3, 1999 which was withheld by Madras High Court on account of 50 per cent reservation to BCs as unconstitutional. The new elected government decided to hold elections without providing reservations to BCs; which finally took place in October 1996.

Conclusion

It is pertinent that if the programmes for rural sanitation and health care are with the panchayats there would be transparency coupled with accessibility, approach, overseeing and administering facilities so essential for a minimum need to be effectively tackled at local levels in a user-friendly culture. It is not whether a particular component of a particular programme in rural sanitation and rural health measures on a State or Central level is relevant to the local needs, it is whether that component is attuned to the specific features of the local situation. It is only the panchayats that can decisively pronounce a verdict on this. It is exactly for this reason that the Eleventh Schedule so elaborately assigns Health and Sanitation to the panchayats.

Further, the district planning mechanism as envisaged under the new dispensation of decentralised planning will accord suitable priorities to individual panchayat needs. In all these, the role of NGOs is also vital. Our field observations have substantiated the view that a satisfactory solution to sanitation and health problems could be found in a "working panchayat". We are optimistic in our conclusion that the 73rd Amendment has tremendous potential in transforming the rural scene to meet people's aspirations and needs adequately.

ANNEXURES

ANNEXURE - I

Government of India, Planning Commission, *Eighth Five-Year Plan: 1992-97*, Vol II, New Delhi.

Government of India, Ministry of Rural Development, *Rural Water Supply and Sanitation Programme in India*, Rajiv Gandhi National Drinking Water Mission, New Delhi, 1993.

Government of India, Ministry of Rural Development, *National Seminar on Rural Sanitation: Problems, Prospects and Strategies for Future*, 16-18 September 1992, New Delhi.

Government of India, Ministry of Rural Development, *General Guidelines for Implementation of Centrally Sponsored Rural Sanitation Programme*, New Delhi, 1993.

Government of India, Planning Commission, *Task-Force: Self-Managed Institutions for Integrated Development*, New Delhi, December 1991.

Government of Uttar Pradesh, Directorate of Panchayati Raj, *Panchayati Raj: Achievement and Progress Report*, Lucknow, 1993-94 and 1994-95.

Operations Research Group, *Evaluation of UNICEF Assisted Programme in Uttar Pradesh: 1984-91*, Lucknow, 1993.

Government of West Bengal, *Intensive Sanitation Project: Progress Report 1993*, Ramakrishna Mission Lokshiksha Parishad, Narendrapur, 1993.

Government of Tamil Nadu, *Periyar District: Report on UNICEF Assisted Project*, Periyar, 1994.

Government of Rajasthan, Department. of Rural Development and Panchayat Raj, *Rajasthan Panchayat Raj Act, 1994-95*, Jaipur.

Government of Orissa, *Rural Sanitation Programme : Puri and Ganjam Districts – Project Report*, Sulabh International, Bhubaneshwar, 1993.

Government of Goa, Public Works Department, *Report on Rural Sanitation Programme for the State of Goa*, Panaji, 1995.

Indian Institute of Rural Management, *Evaluation of Completed Sanitary Facilities Under Rural Sanitation Programme in Rajasthan: A Report*, Jaipur, 1991.

M. S. Swaminathan Research Foundation, *Annual Reports: 1991-92 and 1993-94*, Madras.

Pathak, Bindeshwar, *Road to Freedom: A Sociological Study on the Abolition of Scavenging in India*, Motilal Banarsidas Publishers Pvt. Ltd., Delhi, 1991.

Sinha, Bakshi D. and Ghosh, A.K., *Evaluation of Low-Cost Sanitation*, Council for Social Development, New Delhi, 1990.

Sinha, Bakshi D. and Ghosh A.K., *Sanitation and Environment: Evaluation of Low-Cost Sanitation in Gujarat*, Council for Social Development, New Delhi, (Second Edition), 1994.

Sinha, Bakshi D., Menon, P.S.K and Ghosh, A.K., *Restoration of Human Dignity: Impact of Development Programmes on Scavengers*, Council for Social Development, New Delhi, 1994.

Sinha, Bakshi D. and Ghosh, A.K., *Evaluation of National Scheme of Liberation and Rehabilitation of Scavengers in Uttar Pradesh*, Council for Social Development, New Delhi, 1994.

Institute of Social Sciences, *Status of Panchayati Raj in the States of India 1994*, Concept Publishing Company, New Delhi, 1995.

Mathew, George, *Panchayati Raj in India: From Legislation to Movement*, Concept Publishing Company, New Delhi, 1994.

UNICEF, *Health and Basic Services: Keys to Development*, New Delhi.

World Bank Cell, Gujarat Water Supply and Sewerage Board and Environmental Sanitation Institute, *Low-Cost Sanitation: Sanitary Latrines in Rural Areas of Gujarat State (IDA Credit No. 1643 IN)* April 1989 to July, 1994, Gandhinagar, Ahmedabad.

World Bank, *Karnataka Rural Water Supply and Environmental Sanitation Project: Credit and Project Summary*, New Delhi.

World Bank, *Maharashtra Water Supply and Environmental Sanitation Project: Credit and Project Summary*, New Delhi.

ANNEXURE - II

LIST OF EXTERNALLY FUNDED PROJECTS

Sl. No.	External Agency	State	Name of Project
1	2	3	4
1.	Netherlands	Andhra Pradesh	AP I AP II AP III
		Gujarat	Gujarat WS UU Santalpur Gujarat WS II Lathi-Liliya Gujarat WS II Sami Harij Gujarat Ghogha RWSS Gujarat Kadi RWSS
		Karnataka	Rural Water Supply Scheme I
		Kerala	Nattika Firka Water Supply Scheme Vakkam Anjengo Water Supply Scheme Mala Water Supply Scheme Koipuram Water Supply Scheme Trikunapuzha Water Supply Scheme Cheriyanadu Water Supply Scheme Kundara Water Supply Scheme Pavaraty Water Supply Scheme
		Uttar Pradesh	UP III UP IV UP V (Phase A) UP V (interim phase) UP VI UP VII & UP VIII
2.	DANIDA	Karnataka	Integrated Rural Sanitation and Water Supply Project
		Kerala	Rural Drinking Water Supply Project
		Orissa	Drinking Water Supply Project Phase IIB Handpump Maintenance System in Orissa

1	2	3	4
		Tamil Nadu	Integrated Rural Sanitation and Water Supply Project
3.	ODA	Maharashtra	Maharashtra Rural Drinking Water Supply Scheme
		Orissa	Rural Water Supply and Sanitation Project
4.	Germany	Madhya Pradesh	Water Supply Project Phase II
		Maharashtra	Rural Water Supply and Piped Sanitation Project
		Rajasthan	Water Supply Project
		West Bengal	Water Supply, Sanitation and Health Education Project
5.	EEC	Andhra Pradesh	Water Supply Project
		Rajasthan	Water Supply Project from Lift Irrigation
			Problematic and Various areas near river Chambal
		Tamil Nadu	Rural Water Supply Scheme
6.	World Bank	Karnataka	Karnataka Water Supply and Environmental Sanitation Project
		Maharashtra	Maharashtra Water Supply and Environmental Sanitation Project
		Punjab	Punjab Water Supply and Environmental Project
		Tamil Nadu	Tamil Nadu Water Supply and Environmental Project
		Uttar Pradesh	UP Water Supply and Environmental Sanitation Project.

Source: Government of India, Ministry of Rural Development, Annual Report 1994-95, p. 129.

ANNEXURE - III

STATEWISE AMOUNT OF ASSISTANCE RELEASED UNDER THE NATIONAL SCHEME OF LIBERATION AND REHABILITATION OF SCAVENGERS AND THEIR DEPENDANTS FROM 1991-92 to 1994-95

(Rs. crores)

Sl. No.	State	1991-92	1992-93	1993-94	1994-95 (Upto Dec. '94)
(1)	(2)	(3)	(4)	(5)	(6)
1.	Andhra Pradesh	2.00	2.55	4.59	0.62
2.	Assam	0.125	2.02	–	
3.	Bihar	3.50	3.13	–	
4.	Gujarat	2.50	1.86	2.00	
5.	Haryana	1.50	1.76	7.14	
6.	Himachal Pradesh	0.60	2.53	–	
7.	Karnataka	1.75	3.99	–	
8.	Kerala	0.25	0.38	–	
9.	Madhya Pradesh	4.00	13.36	12.26	13.80
10.	Maharashtra	3.70	6.59	3.78	
11.	Orissa	3.50	0.58	1.19	
12.	Punjab	3.50	0.58	–	
13.	Rajasthan	4.75	1.01	2.27	
14.	Tamil Nadu	5.00	0.80	–	2.44
15.	Uttar Pradesh	8.00	14.94	37.63	30.05
16.	West Bengal	2.00	3.63	–	
17.	Delhi	3.75	0.05	–	
18.	Pondicherry	0.025	0.05		
19.	Nagaland	–	–	0.11	
20.	J & K	0.025	1.00		
21.	Meghalaya	0.025	–	–	
Total		50.50	60.73	70.97	6.91

Source: Government of India, Ministry of Welfare, Annual Report, 1994 -95, p.132.

ANNEXURE - IV

STATEWISE PROGRESS MADE UNDER THE NATIONAL SCHEME OF LIBERATION AND REHABILITATION OF SCAVENGERS AND THEIR DEPENDENTS

Sl. No.	State/UT	No. of Scavengers Identified	Progress Made During			
			1992-93		1993-94	
			Trained	Rehabilitated	Trained	Rehabilitated
(1)	(2)	(3)	(4)	(5)	(6)	(7)
1.	Andhra Pradesh	7453	–	989	500	2556
2.	Assam	5651	–	–	–	–
3.	Bihar	40249	–	–	–	–
4.	Gujarat	40000	–	623	–	973
5.	Haryana	18488	–	–	888	1295
6.	Himachal Pradesh	4760	115	10	151	123
7.	Jammu & Kashmir	3548	–	–	275	–
8.	Karnataka	5825	–	–	166	107
9.	Kerala	1339	86	–	144	116
10.	Madhya Pradesh	80072	11395	10194	19892	12383
11.	Maharashtra	126691	1248	1675	644	2792
12.	Orissa	17122	209	26	1080	805
13.	Punjab	26819	130	–	4102	1138
14.	Rajasthan	87938	528	178	2147	1543
15.	Tamil Nadu	35561	–	–	–	2556
16.	Uttar Pradesh	226189	1868	4620	1065	15213
17.	West Bengal	30000	–	–	103	–
18.	Delhi	17420	–	505	13	–
19.	Pondicherry	476	–	93	–	93
20.	Nagaland	1800	–	–	–	–
	Total	7,36,114	15,579	18,913	22,115	41,950

Source: Government of India, Ministry of Welfare, Annual Report, 1994-95, p.133.

INDEX